MW01205751

Help!
I NEED AN
Idea

JAMES E. TAULMAN

BROADMAN PRESS
Nashville, Tennessee

4234-32

ISBN: 0-8054-3432-1

Dewey Decimal Classification: 268.6
Subject Heading: TEACHING // DEVOTIONAL LITERATURE
Library of Congress Catalog Card Number: 86-20787
Printed in the United States of America

Library of Congress Cataloging-in-Publication Data

Taulman, James E., 1937-
  Help! : I need an idea.

  Includes indexes.
  1. Drama in Christian education. I. Title.
BV1534.4.T34   1987   268'.6   86-20787
ISBN 0-8054-3432-1 (soft)

Foreword

James Taulman has succeeded in doing what the title of his book suggests—he has provided considerable help for pastors, other staff members, and lay persons. He has given us scores of creative and interesting ways of presenting the gospel.

With a rich background of experience in preaching and editing, Taulman provides ready to use and practical biblical skits, biblical readings, and simulations. Monologues and pantomimes are to be found as well. A potpourri of ideas such as life situations, case studies, twenty questions, and various puzzles and games provide additional stimulating and helpful ways to creatively present the timeless gospel. I believe James Taulman's book will find ready acceptance and wide use. It is a book to be kept close at hand. Its uses are almost endless. It is a practical, useful, and easy to use book. If you need helpful, creative ideas in presenting the gospel, this book is a must for you.

HARRY PILAND

Contents

1

Help! I Need an Idea

Have you ever said, "I'd give five dollars for a good idea"? Here is a whole book of ideas for devotionals, Sunday School lessons, and Bible studies, and all for about that proverbial five dollars. If you have ever had the responsibility of teaching a Bible study, leading a worship service, or giving a devotional and felt like you needed an idea to get started, here's help. Sunday School lessons and other presentations of the gospel do not have to be burdensome to prepare. Nor do they have to be dull and boring. They can come alive! Most church leaders have the ability to make the gospel come alive, but they often need help. Providing that help is one of the purposes of this book.

This book gives you material to use just as it is printed. You can look up a Scripture or topic in the Index and find something that you can use to help you present an effective program, devotional, or lesson. If you are not trying to support a particular Scripture or theme, your choices are made even greater. You can skim through the book and find a feature that will communicate to your audience.

However, the book has another function. I'm convinced that you can do more than simply use these as they are printed if you are willing to take the time. You can also learn to develop some creative methods of presenting the gospel. It will take some time, but learning to develop creative ways of presenting the gospel will help you proclaim the greatest truths in the world in a way that is worthy. The chapter on "Steps in Developing Creative Teaching Methods" will give you ideas about how to write your own creative materials. Also, each chapter has specific suggestions to help you prepare particular features.

Ways to Use This Book

This book has a dozen or more uses. The different ways the ideas in this book can be used are limited only by you. Most of the features are brief enough that they can be used in the context of a Sunday School class. They can be used to create interest in Bible study, to make Bible study purposeful, to apply biblical truth to life. They can be used to survey long passages of Scripture, to show class members how the Bible relates to their lives today, and to get members of classes to come to grips with what the Bible means if they take it seriously. Let me illustrate how this might be done. Let's assume that the Sunday School lesson is about the good Samaritan (Luke 10:25-37). Look in the Index under that Scripture reference. Several options are available. If you have a departmental period or opening assembly, use "A Funny Thing Happened on the Way to Jericho" to create interest and provide a springboard for the class discussion. Use one of the life situation experiences about a person needing help, and at the conclusion ask one of the members to summarize the parable by miming it. You could devise a crossword puzzle of key words from the parable to have on the chairs as members arrive.

The more you use these ideas in teaching the Bible, the more you will discover how you can use them in other ways.

Do you need an idea for a devotional? Right at your fingertips you have access to several dozen features that can be used as devotions at women's meetings, missionary meetings, deacons' meetings, civic clubs, Sunday School class meetings, retreats, or any place you would give a devotional. These are new ideas and new forms; the people to whom you speak have not heard them before. You will be able to communicate the old, old story in a new way. The message is timeless; the medium must be timely.

As more lay people exercise their precious privilege and responsibility of the priesthood of the believer, they are becoming involved in leading worship services. Here's help for that too. Whether you are leading a service on a special day in your church, or whether you are conducting a worship service in the absence of a pastor, many of the ideas in this book will help you. Several of the longer biblical skits can be adapted as pulpit dramas. Use one of the hymn ideas and one or two of the biblical skits as the sermon, bathe those ideas in prayer, and God can use them for His glory.

Pastors also can find help here. Instead of reading the Scripture before preaching, use a biblical skit or a biblical reading to present to the congregation the biblical facts that are contained in the Scripture. Attempts have been made to include in the biblical skits as many of the pertinent facts as possible in each section of Scripture used. If you are going to preach on Jesus at the wedding feast in Cana (John 2:1-11), you can use "They Have No Wine" instead of reading the Scripture. Enlist three persons to help you read the text. The message will be communicated, but some will grasp its meaning more easily because you have used a different way of presenting it.

The time references given for each feature are only approximate. Several factors can affect the time it will take to present a feature. The time is given only as a general guide to help you in your planning.

Study the layout of this book. Become familiar with it so you can use it to the best advantages. It will provide creative ideas for teaching the Bible and presenting the gospel.

Props and Dress

What about dressing in biblical outfits and using props when presenting these activities? My personal feeling is that wearing biblical dress is not necessary—especially in a Sunday School classroom. Dressing in biblical dress takes too much energy for the benefit gained. People have fertile imaginations; let them use them.

However, where you are using the learning activity and your purpose in using it may help you decide to use biblical outfits and props. If you are using a monologue or a biblical skit for a worship service or as a devotional for a large meeting, the extra effort might be worth it. Just do not let the use of props and dress detract from what you want to accomplish. Be sure that whatever you do enhances rather than takes away from the message you are presenting.

Another question you need to answer is whether to memorize the material. Normally the answer is no. Memorization requires too much effort for the benefit gained. Reading the activity can be just as effective as memorizing it.

However, certain occasions may merit memorization—especially if the presenter(s) memorizes easily and you plan to use the activity more than once. The rule of simplicity applies here too.

Stage Directions

Few stage directions have been included. You are encouraged to study the features enough that you "feel" what you should do. You can add movement, voice inflection, laughter. You can position people in the front of the room, the sides of the room, the back of the room, or scatter them throughout the congregation. In some cases ("Father Forgive Them") readers may be out of sight. Readers can face the audience all the time or they can turn their backs when not speaking. Staging can add a lot to the message. However, there is no particular right way to do each activity. How you present a biblical skit may change from time to time, depending on where you present it and the particular effect you want to achieve, and each presentation can be equally effective.

What About Copies?

In any book of this nature, the question arises about copies. Most of the activities require two or more people, each of whom needs a copy of the script. Does this mean you need to buy a book for each person? Or can you put it on your trusty copy machine and zip off the copies you need? Well, . . . yes and no. Yes to the first question and no to the second. This material is copyrighted and cannot legally be reproduced without permission of the publisher.

I hope you enjoy using the material in this book as much as I have enjoyed putting it together. My own creative powers have been challenged and expanded. But aside from that stimulus, I have looked at the Scriptures in a new light. As I have tried to make them come alive for you, they have also come alive for me. I have gained new insights from the Scriptures I have used. My prayer is that as you use these activities and learn to develop your own you will understand anew how fresh and vital God's Word is.

2

Steps in Developing
Creative Ways to Present the Gospel

Can any church leader develop creative ways to present the gospel? Yes and no. It all depends on what level of complexity one wants to achieve. Anyone can develop a biblical reading of a Scripture passage. In fact, that is the way many classes are (poorly) taught each Sunday morning. "Bob, you read the first verse and tell us what it means. Bill, you read the second verse and tell us what it means." The teacher has assigned verses to be read by people in a given order. That is a biblical reading in its simplest form. However, with a little more thought and preparation, the reading will accomplish more than this haphazard approach.

This chapter will provide you with some general guidelines for developing creative ways to present the gospel. Of course, a certain amount of creativity is required, but many people have creativity that is completely untapped. Following these suggestions can help you stimulate your own creative juices.

Study the Scripture Thoroughly

The first step is to study the Scripture thoroughly. The Scripture must come alive for you, or it will not come alive for your class. This, of course, applies to all levels of Bible study. Read the passage. Consult other translations. Read commentaries. Be sure you understand what the biblical writer was trying to communicate. A thorough knowledge of Scripture is a must for developing any kind of method to present its truth.

You are not rewriting Scripture. You are interpreting it. Throughout His ministry, Jesus often used parables. The parable was normally a story (although not always) that communicated in a clear way some point Jesus wanted to make. Often these points had been made in the Old

Testament Scriptures. The parable of the good Samaritan is a moving story that was remembered by most who heard it. However, the basic idea of the story is found in many passages throughout the Old Testament. "The Lord has told us what is good. What he requires of us is this: to do what is just, to show constant love, and to live in humble fellowship with our God" (Mic. 6:8, GNB). Jesus took an idea in the Old Testament and couched it in story form.

Preachers do the same thing in preaching. They constantly seek illustrations to communicate biblical truth. We remember a pithy illustration or story longer than we remember abstract truth. Your group or class members will too.

Biblical truth remains unchanged through the ages. We need always to be on the lookout for new ways to present that changeless truth. That's why it is imperative that you saturate yourself in the Scripture before you attempt to use any method to present the Scripture's message.

Decide What You Want to Accomplish

What do you want to accomplish? What are you trying to communicate? What is the best way of doing it? What kind of setting do you need? How many people will you have available to help you, and how many will you have in the class or group? All of these facts should be considered.

Some passages of Scripture lend themselves to certain forms better than others. Look at the passage and try to let it dictate which form you use to communicate your message. An eighteen-wheeler can move a small box across town, but it can be done far more efficiently in a car or small truck. Be sure the expression fits the Scripture.

In deciding what you want to accomplish, you will also be deciding to some extent what kind of form you will use. Do you want to present the Scripture for your class to listen to and then discuss? If so, a biblical reading would suffice.

Do you want the class to discover certain facts in a large amount of background Scripture? A word puzzle of some type would lead them to discover this. A crossword puzzle or a word search puzzle can help members get into the Scripture and discover many facts for themselves. You have the opportunity to direct which facts they discover by how you construct the puzzle.

Do you want to use the Scripture to communicate a certain message? If so, a biblical skit that expands the text or lifts certain verses and groups them together will help you accomplish your goal.

Do you want members to experience a biblical passage and see how it relates to their lives today? Use a biblical simulation in which you ask members to imagine or simulate the biblical scene.

Do you want to convey the feelings of the people in the Bible? If so, write a monologue to communicate the feelings of the biblical characters as you understand them.

Start Early

Don't wait until the last minute to begin developing a special form. It does take time. It might be possible to compose a biblical reading on Saturday night for your class to use the next morning, but most forms will take more time.

Experiment with Forms

It may take a little practice to decide which form will best communicate the particular information you want to share with your group. Consult the charts on the following pages. The information given will help you decide. Of course, nearly any form can be used to accomplish any purpose. It all depends on how you develop it.

Let Your Imagination Run

Give free rein to your imagination. If you are developing a monologue, try to think like the biblical person you are portraying. Imagine what he or she must have felt in the particular situation. A good way of doing this is to ask, If this person had kept a detailed diary, what would be written in it about this event? Another way would be to identify people in the early church or Bible with people today. For example, many of today's petty, cruel dictators are similar to some of the rulers in the Bible who were so insecure. You can visualize a modern-day person and ascribe some of the same characteristics to a character in the Bible.

Learning Activities and Desired Outcome	
Desired Outcome	**Suggested Activity[1]**
Knowledge (gather additional information)	biblical skits, crossword puzzles, word search puzzles, biblical readings, case studies, pulpit drama, pantomime
Understanding (application of information)	case studies, biblical skits, monologues, biblical simulations, hymn activities, pantomime
Skills (incorporation of new ways performing through practice)	case studies, life situations
Attitudes and Values (adoption of new feelings and perspectives)	case studies, life situations, pantomimes

1. Many of these activities can be used to achieve different outcomes, depending on how they are constructed.

Purpose or Aim	Create Learning Readiness	Make Bible Study Purposeful	1. Explore Background Information	2. Overview Long Bible Passages	3. Read Bible Passage	4. Discover What the Bible Means	Get Bible Truth into Life		Using Creative Ways to Present the Gospel
	X		X					Word Search Puzzles	
			X			X		Twenty Questions	
	X		X					Crossword Puzzles	
	X		X	X	X	X	X	Biblical Skits	
				X		X		Biblical Simulation	
	X						X	Case Studies	
	X					X	X	Monologues	
	X			X		X	X	Pulpit Drama	
	X				X			Biblical Readings	
	X					X	X	Life Situations	
	X					X	X	Hymn Activities	
	X						X	Pantomime	

Enlist People to Help You

Some of these learning methods do not require practice or preparation on the part of the group members. Crossword puzzles, games, and biblical readings do not need any kind of preparation by those using them. However, monologues, biblical skits, and biblical simulations do require some practice to use them well. Of course, this will depend on your class or group and how you plan to use the activity.

In most cases it will be best to enlist people to help you in advance of the time you plan to use them. If you ask people in advance, they will feel more comfortable. You can involve people who might not otherwise say much in a discussion in the class. If you have enough people, you can use more than one reader for each voice in a choral reading. This will encourage persons who are hesitant to participate.

Keep It Simple

Keep what you are doing simple. You are not writing a script for a movie; you are writing a learning activity to use in just one step or part of a step in your total teaching plan or program. It doesn't have to be elaborate and complicated to be effective. Keep the use of props to a minimum or eliminate them entirely. The less complicated your forms are the less need there will be for practice. Also, the less complicated the form, the fewer things can go wrong.

You will experience exceptions. You may want to develop a program that will take more time and need more preparation. A biblical simulation and a pulpit drama are examples. If you use these forms, you certainly would want to assign roles a week in advance. That way group members would have time to study and research their roles.

Keep a File

After you have developed a particular activity, be sure you keep it. Don't throw it away. If it worked, you may want to use it again. If it did not work, you will want to make some notes about what went wrong and how you can change it for the future. A flop may be of more help to you in the long run than a success. Some of the features in this book have gone through many stages as I found what would work and what would not.

File your ideas and keep an index of them. Index them by Scripture and topic, as I have done in this book. It is surprising how many times you can use them in different ways. You might submit some of your better pieces for publication. Periodicals that deal with Sunday School workers might consider printing them.

Keep Trying

Don't give up if one of your creative ideas turned out not to be so creative. You're not the first person who has had a failure. Keep trying. Analyze why it didn't work, and make some notes on it immediately. Was the aim clear? What did you hope to accomplish? Was it too complicated? Did you need more practice? Was it written early enough to give you time to prepare it?

Whatever you do, don't quit. Keep trying. Remember that even the best athletes do not score every time. Church leaders are allowed to fail once in a while too.

Be Sure the Message Is Not Lost in the Medium

A word of caution: Be sure that the message you are trying to communicate to your class is not lost in the medium. I once saw a woman in a grocery store who was dressed in an absolutely stunning outfit. She had on a red suit, red hat, and red accessories. She was dressed quite nicely. However, when I tried later to remember her face, I could not. Her clothing had detracted from her looks.

Don't let your vehicle detract from the cargo it is carrying. The cargo, not the vehicle, is the important element. One way to do this is to keep your purpose clearly in mind. Set your goal and aim toward it. Test everything by that aim or goal.

Finally, Brethren and Sisters

All of this takes so much time and energy and ability you say. Sure it does! But you are involved in the greatest teaching program in the world—the teaching of God's Word. It deserves your very best.

You are already giving a lot of time each week in your study and preparation or you wouldn't be reading this book. With just a little more time and energy, you can present the gospel in an exciting way. A speaker in a chapel service in college said he was thirty-six years old before he ever started to college. People said, "Man, you're crazy. You'll be forty years old when you graduate." He said, "Well, I looked at it this way. In four years I was going to be forty anyway. I might as well be forty with a college education as forty without it."

You give a great deal of time already. You are going to be teaching week after week. You might as well make the class come alive as to let it sleep through a study of the most important Book in the world.

3

Biblical Skits

Biblical skits can be fun! They can present a great deal of biblical information in an enjoyable way. They have a versatility that allows them to be used in many different ways.

The biblical skits in this book are designed for two to seven people. Most of them require two or three readers. They are designed to be read. A person who is a good reader should be able to read over the skit once or twice and then present it. However, a rehearsal would improve the presentation.

Different types of skits are included. Some are composed mostly of Scripture ("A Life Worthy of Your Calling"). Some do not quote any Scripture ("Perfectly Good Pigs") but are a retelling of the events record- ed in Scripture from someone else's viewpoint. All of them convey information that the Bible contains and can be used as discussion start- ers, to create interest at the beginning of a Bible study, or as devotionals. Those with a missions theme can be used in missionary meetings.

You can put two or three of these skits together with some biblical readings and develop a worship service. The following is an example.

The Life of Jesus

His Birth	Biblical reading on Matthew 2:1-12
His Ministry	But It's the Sabbath
	A biblical skit based on John 5:1-9
His Death	Father, Forgive Them
	A biblical skit based on Luke 23:34
His Resurrection	An Unusual Thing Happened on the Road to Emmaus
	A biblical skit between Cleopas and his wife Mary

His Commission

Our Affirmation

Based on Luke 24:13-32
Go Ye Therefore
A biblical skit based on Matthew 28:19-20
The Lord Our God Is One Lord
Based on Deuteronomy 6:4
(The middle section relating to Jesus)

This kind of arrangement can illustrate how you can put several of these biblical skits together and use them for worship services. Try your own arrangement by checking the index for topics and Scriptures.

If you cannot find a biblical skit on a particular topic you want, try writing your own. To help you understand the process I go through in writing, let me share with you an analysis of "They Have No Wine."

- Be certain that nothing in the skit is contrary to biblical fact. Some extrabiblical facts are in the skit but nothing is contrary to the Bible or would lead someone to believe something happened in the Bible that did not actually happen.

- Use a refrain. A refrain can help tie the skit together and even give the skit its title as in this case. The refrain, "They have no wine" has a double meaning and is changed slightly at the conclusion to help the skit make its application. Refrains are helpful to use in this type of skit. However, they can also communicate something you do not want communicated. I did not intend for this refrain to be humorous. However, in the original skit I had the refrain inserted in the third and fifth lines. But it was too much. People often snickered or even laughed when the first reader would read the line so many times, so I took them out. It works much better in its present form. Be certain that the person reading the refrain understands the purpose of the refrain. It is the most difficult of all parts to read.

- Explanation of biblical facts can be included in the skit. For example, two phrases help explain the biblical passage: "Twenty to thirty gallons" explains the King James Version statement, "two or three firkins." The expression "purification rites" explains "after the manner of the purifying of the Jews." If you have difficult passages or expressions, a biblical skit enables you to explain these.

- You can also use biblical skits to make interpretations of your own. In this case, the biblical text has already said that this event was a miracle. By using the expression, "that would require a miracle," I have affirmed my own belief in that fact that what Jesus did was, indeed, miraculous.

- Biblical skits can also use application. This is something that the Bible by itself does not always do. That is why preachers preach sermons and Bible teachers teach. You have the opportunity to apply the biblical text. "Could He take my life and give me newness?" involves both application and interpretation. The phrase indicates that, as far as I understand the miracle, Jesus is offering newness to those who will follow Him. That offer of newness also keeps the biblical skit from being just a record of what is in the Bible. You can apply the Scripture to the lives of the people who hear it.

- You can even move to action in a skit. In the phrase, "Lord, *we* have no wine," the two bystanders in the skit move from simply observing what Jesus has done to being personally involved. The Bible is, in the final analysis, about you and me. Jesus is not only talking about people in the first century but also about us today. Whatever you write, you must find some way to involve the people in some kind of action or response. This is the invitation that calls people to decision for Christ.

- The skit is written from the position of two onlookers. Although these onlookers are not mentioned in the Bible, their presence does no violence to the biblical text. These two people give an opportunity to express some of the feelings and attitudes that we (or others) have about the biblical passage. They express questions about the miracle that people through the ages have raised. However, in the final analysis, they move from being antagonistic to being convinced that Jesus really did turn water into wine. They ask Him to work His miracle in their lives just as He did with the water and wine.

- Throughout the skit I have used my imagination. I have tried to put myself in the position of people looking at the miracle who previously did not believe in Jesus. Then I moved through the feelings they might have had about what was going on and came to the place where the onlookers affirmed the need of Jesus' power in their own lives.

- The skit can be read in two or three minutes. It is brief enough to be used in a Bible study or as a substitute for a Scripture reading in a worship service. Yet, it is long enough to present the facts of the Scripture passage. At times you may want a longer skit, but length is not an assurance of a good skit. Let the Scripture dictate the length of the skit.

• Try to assign certain personalities to various voices. Although the voices in "They Have No Wine" do not necessarily demonstrate this principle, many of the other skits do. Just as characters in a play or novel have certain personalities, try to develop your voices in this same way. Voice 3 in "Go Ye Therefore" is a cynical, questioning type. Voice 1 in "Perfectly Good Pigs" is typical of a person who tries to turn a situation to his own advantage. We have all met people like that. We have also met people like Voice 2 in "But It's the Sabbath" who are more concerned about rules and regulations than about people's needs. Although you do not have a lot of space and time to develop your personalities, you can do a great deal in the space and time you have.

The Seven Days of Creation

Scripture Reference: Genesis 1:1 to 2:3
Voices: 5
Time: 12 minutes

The First Day of Creation

1: "In the beginning God created the heaven and the earth.
2: "And the earth was without form,
1: "and void;
2: "and darkness
3:              darkness
1:                    darkness
2: "was upon the face of the deep.
ALL (*softly*): "And the spirit of God moved upon the face of the waters.
2: "And God said,
3: "Let there be
ALL: "light:
1: "and there was light.

2: "And God saw the light, that it was good:
1: "And God divided the light from the darkness.
1 & 2: "And God called the light Day,
2 (*softly*): "and the darkness he called Night.
1: "And the evening and the morning were the first day."

ANTAGONIST: Aha! I've got you! You said God created the world? Who created God?
PROTAGONIST: God is. He has always existed. In the beginning He was already there. No one created Him. He alone is the Creator.
ANTAGONIST: But who created God? I cannot believe in a world created by someone I do not understand. We moderns want fact. I accept only that which I can explain. None of this mystical stuff for me.
PROTAGONIST: I see. You accept only that which you can explain?
ANTAGONIST: That's right.
PROTAGONIST: OK, would you explain love for me?
ANTAGONIST: But, . . . but, that's different. You're comparing apples and oranges.
PROTAGONIST: Possibly, but some things can't be explained. Some things can't be analyzed and put in a test tube. Some things just have to be accepted . . . on faith.

The Second Day of Creation

2: "And God said,
3: "Let there be a firmament in the midst of the waters, and let it divide the waters from the waters.
2: "And God made the firmament,
1: "And divided the waters which were under the firmament from the waters which were above the firmament:
2: "And it was so.
ALL: "And God called the firmament Heaven.
1: "And the evening and the morning were the second day."

ANTAGONIST: Aw, come on now. Surely you don't expect me to believe that's the way God created the world. Why, that just sounds like a lot of myth and pious religious talk.
PROTAGONIST: Do you have a better suggestion?
ANTAGONIST: Well, personally I subscribe to the big bang theory. All

of the gas molecules got together and there was a big explosion and the earth came out of that.

PROTAGONIST: Sounds interesting. Who made the gas molecules?

ANTAGONIST: Well, they formed from . . . well, uh . . . I still think there must be a better explanation than that God did it.

PROTAGONIST: I prefer to believe that God created the world than that it happened accidentally.

The Third Day of Creation

2: "And God said,

3: "Let the waters under the heaven be gathered together unto one place, and let the dry land appear:

2: "And it was so.

1: "And God called the dry land

2 & 3: "Earth;

1: "And the gathering together of the waters called he

2 & 3: "Seas:

1: "And God saw that it was good.

2: "And God said,

3: "Let the earth bring forth grass, the herb yielding seed, and the fruit tree yielding fruit after his kind, whose seed is in itself, upon the earth:

2: And it was so.

1: And the earth brought forth grass,

2: And herb yielding seed after his kind,

1 & 3: And the tree yielding fruit, whose seed was in itself, after his kind:

2: And God saw that it was good.

1: "And the evening and the morning were the third day."

PROTAGONIST: Well, what do you think?

ANTAGONIST: Hmm. I *had* always thought that life began in the sea. That seems to be the consensus of the best scientific minds of the past several generations.

PROTAGONIST: That's nice.

ANTAGONIST: Their contention is that life began in the ocean, and then as the water began to recede from the earth, life began to form on the earth.

PROTAGONIST: I see. Tell me more.

ANTAGONIST: First, there would have been small plants, then larger ones, until finally there were trees.

PROTAGONIST: You mean just like the Bible says. That's interesting.

ANTAGONIST: Well, I . . . er . . . I guess so.

The Fourth Day of Creation

2: "And God said,

3: "Let there be lights in the firmament of the heaven to divide the day from the night; and let them be for signs, and for seasons, and for days, and years: And let them be for lights in the firmament of the heaven to give light upon the earth:

2: "And it was so.

1: "And God made two great lights;

2: "The greater light to rule the day,

1: "And the lesser light to rule the night:

2 & 3: "He made the stars also.

2: "And God set them in the firmament of the heaven

1: "to give light upon the earth,

2: "And to rule over the day and over the night,

1: "and to divide the light from the darkness:

2: "and God saw that it was good.

1: "And the evening and the morning were the fourth day."

ANTAGONIST: There you go again. Two lights? Even the youngest schoolchild knows that the moon is not a light. It simply reflects the light of the sun. What do you have to say about that?

PROTAGONIST: Everyone knows that the moon is not a light?

ANTAGONIST: That's right. Everybody.

PROTAGONIST: Let me ask you a question. Do you like to play games?

ANTAGONIST: Games? I haven't time for such frivolity. We have serious matters to discuss, and you want to play games. Just answer my question.

PROTAGONIST: Oh, I am going to answer your question. Or rather you are going to answer it yourself. Quickly now, the game won't take long. All you have to do is complete the sentence by adding one word. Are you ready?

ANTAGONIST: Oh, all right. Just to humor you.

PROTAGONIST: Fine. Let's go. These are song titles. Fill in the missing word. "By the (*blank*) of the Silvery Moon."

ANTAGONIST (*hesitantly*): "Light."

PROTAGONIST: "In the Misty Moon (*blank*)."

ANTAGONIST: "Light."

PROTAGONIST: "Moon (*blank*) Sonata."

ANTAGONIST (*beginning to catch on*): "Light." OK, OK, but you really haven't proved anything.

PROTAGONIST: I know. All I have done is to show you that people who do know that the moon is not a light still refer to it as a light. I grant you that the biblical writers may not have known what we know today, but it is hard not to think of the moon as a light on a clear night when it is full. Give them a little poetic license, just like you do the songwriters today.

ANTAGONIST: Well, I'm still not convinced.

The Fifth Day of Creation

2: "And God said,

3: "Let the waters bring forth abundantly the moving creature that hath life, and fowl that may fly above the earth in the open firmament of heaven.

1: "And God created great whales,

2: "And every living creature that moveth, which the waters brought forth abundantly, after their kind,

1: "And every winged fowl after his kind:

2: "And God saw that it was good.

1: "And God blessed them, saying,

3: "Be fruitful, and multiply, and fill the waters in the seas, and let fowl multiply in the earth.

1: "And the evening and the morning were the fifth day."

ANTAGONIST (*silence*)

PROTAGONIST: I don't hear anything from you.

ANTAGONIST: I was just thinking.

PROTAGONIST: Care to share your thoughts?

ANTAGONIST: Well, I'm not quite sure. I'm really confused. Just give me some time to think through all of this. You've laid some heavy stuff on me.

PROTAGONIST: All right.

The Sixth Day of Creation

2: "And God said,

3: "Let the earth bring forth the living creature after his kind, cattle, and creeping thing, and beast of the earth after his kind:

1: "And it was so.

2: "And God made the beast of the earth after his kind,

1: "And cattle after their kind,

2: "And every thing that creepeth upon the earth after his kind.

1: "And God saw that it was good.

2: "And God said,

ALL: "Let us make man in our image, after our likeness: And let them have dominion

2: "over the fish of the sea,

3: "And over the fowl of the air,

1: "And over the cattle,

2: "And over all the earth,

3: "And over every creeping thing that creepeth upon the earth.

1: "So God created man in his own image.

1 & 2: "In the image of God created he him.

2: "Male

1: "And Female

1 & 2: "Created he them.

2: "And God blessed them, and God said unto them,

3: "Be fruitful, and multiply, and replenish the earth, and subdue it: and have dominion over the fish of the sea, and over the fowl of the air, and over every living thing that moveth upon the earth.

2: "And God said,

3: "Behold I have given you every herb bearing seed, which is upon the face of all the earth, and every tree, in the which is the fruit of a tree yielding seed; to you it shall be for meat. And to every beast of the earth, and to every fowl of the air, and to every thing that creepeth upon the earth, wherein there is life, I have given every green herb for meat:

1: "And it was so.

2: "And God saw every thing that he had made, and, behold, it was very good.

1: "And the evening and the morning were the sixth day."

ANTAGONIST: So that's how we got here? It does make sense.

PROTAGONIST: I'm surprised to hear you say that.

ANTAGONIST: Well, I surprised myself. But I had just never thought of it that way before. It really is a beautiful story, isn't it?

PROTAGONIST: Yes, it is. But it is more than just a story. It is God's way of telling us that He is concerned about us. He made us in His image, and we can never be at peace with ourselves until we are at peace with Him.

ANTAGONIST: You mean this emptiness in my life can be filled with God?

PROTAGONIST: Yes, God has made an emptiness in our lives in His shape and only He can fill that space.

The Seventh Day of Creation

2: "Thus the heavens and the earth were finished,

1 & 2: "And all the host of them.

2: "And on the seventh day God ended his work which he had made;

1: "And he rested on the seventh day from all his work which he had made.

1 & 2: "And God blessed the seventh day,

2: "And sanctified it:

1: "Because that in it he had rested from all his work which God created and made."

ANTAGONIST: Is . . . God . . . really through with creation?

PROTAGONIST: Why do you ask?

ANTAGONIST: I wonder if He could take my emptiness and create something out of it? Could He take my confusion and bring order to it?

PROTAGONIST: That's the good news. God never ceases making old lives new. He did it long ago with the world, and He has continued to do it with every life since then that has opened itself and let Him speak the word of creation. He offers a new beginning to everyone.

ANTAGONIST (*looking up to heaven*): In . . . the . . . beginning . . . God!

ALL (*except Antagonist*): And God said, That's good!

The Lord Our God Is One Lord

Scripture Reference: Deuteronomy 6:4
Voices: 3
Time: 2:30

1: "The *Lord* our God is one Lord."
2: "I believe in God the Father Almighty, maker of heaven and earth."[1]
3: Who called Abraham from among the unbelievers and brought him
   into the Land of Promise,
2: Who created a great people and sheltered them and cared for them
   by sending them into Egypt;
3: Who brought His people out of Egypt with many wonders and signs;
2: Who from Sinai's lofty heights gave His people laws to live by;
3: Who established the lineage of David to rule and promised him he
   would always have a descendant as king.
2 & 3: Yes, we believe in God.

1: "The Lord our *God* is one Lord."
2: "I believe in Jesus Christ His only Son our Lord: who was conceived
   by the Holy Spirit, born of the Virgin Mary, suffered under Pontius
   Pilate, was crucified, dead, and buried; the third day He rose from
   the dead; he ascended into heaven, and sitteth at the right hand of
   the Father Almighty; from thence he shall come to judge the quick
   and the dead."[2]
3: I believe in Jesus because I have met Him and know Him to be real.
2: I believe in Him, not just because He is a historical person, but I believe
   in Him because He alone is able to remove my sin and let me stand
   before the Holy God uncondemned.
3: I believe in Him because I have seen Him change lives of women and
   men.
2: I believe in Him because I have seen Him give children and youth a
   sense of direction for their lives.
3: I believe in Him because He is alive and lives within my heart.
2 & 3: Yes, we believe in Jesus.

1: "The Lord our God is *one* Lord."
2: "I believe in the Holy Spirit, the Lord, the giver of life, who proceedeth

from the Father and the Son, who with the Father and the Son together is worshiped and glorified, who spoke by the prophets."[3]

3: I believe in the Holy Spirit because I have felt His convicting power in my life.

2: I believe in the Holy Spirit because He has convicted me of my sin and showed me my need for a Savior.

3: I believe in the Holy Spirit because I have received from Him guidance and leadership when I did not know the way to go.

2: I believe in the Holy Spirit because He offers encouragement and strength when I am weak.

3: I believe in the Holy Spirit because He is able to take that which I cannot voice and lay my request before the throne of God and interpret it in His presence.

2 & 3: Yes, we believe in the Holy Spirit.

1: "The Lord our God is one *Lord.*"

ALL: Hallelujah!

Notes

    1. *The Apostles' Creed.*
    2. *The Apostles' Creed.*
    3. *The Nicene Creed.*

Go Ye Therefore

Scripture Reference: Matthew 28:19-20
Voices: 4
Time: 2:15

1: "*Go* ye therefore, and teach all nations. . . ."

2: Are we really to do that?

3: Naw, that's just a command Jesus gave to His disciples thousands of years ago. It doesn't apply to us.

4: Are you sure?

1: "Go *ye* therefore, and teach all nations. . . ."

2: That sounds pretty positive.

3: Don't let a little statement like that ripped out of context bother you. If people want to hear about God, they know where the churches are.

4: Are you sure?

1: "Go ye therefore, and *teach* all nations. . . ."

2: If that statement isn't true, and we don't have to go, what about the last part of the verse that promises Christ will be with us until the end of the world? Does that mean it isn't true either?

3: Well, . . . not exactly. Some statements in the Bible are intended to be taken literally. But it's obvious Jesus never meant for us to go to all the world and preach the gospel. Why, the world's a big place! He just couldn't have meant that.

4: Are you sure?

1: "Go ye therefore, and teach *all* nations. . . ."

2: I just really feel this verse applies to me. But I don't know exactly what to do about it.

3: Well, even if it still does apply to this day and age, it doesn't apply to us. It's just for professional missionaries who go to foreign countries.

4: Are you sure?

1: "Go ye therefore, and teach all *nations.* . . ."

2: Could this mean that each of us is to take the gospel into the worlds to which we go? Some to foreign countries, some to their "worlds" of influence, but all are intended to be witnesses?

3: Well, it sort of sounds like that, but I'm sure if we understood the original language we could be able to grasp the meaning of this verse.

4: Are you sure?

1: "Go ye therefore, and teach all nations, baptizing them in the name of the Father, and of the Son, and of the Holy Ghost: Teaching them to observe all things whatsoever I have commanded you: and, lo, I am with you alway, even unto the end of the world. Amen."

4: I'm sure.

Over the Waves

Scripture References: Mark 6:45-52 (Matt. 14:22-33; John 6:16-21)
Voices: 2
Time: 6:15

MARK: Peter, tell me again about the time Jesus walked on the water. That still seems so hard to believe.

PETER: But Mark, I have already told you that story.

MARK: I know, but if I am going to write a complete account of Jesus' life, I must be sure I have all my facts straight.

PETER: OK. It was hard for me to believe it when it happened. In fact, I didn't believe it.

MARK: But you didn't really question whether Jesus could do it, did you?

PETER: Oh, no! That wasn't even the point. We—I—knew Jesus could do anything He wanted to do. It was just . . . well . . . He had never done anything like that before.

MARK: Start at the beginning so I can get it all down.

PETER: Well, we had crossed over to the eastern side of the lake with Jesus. We had gone there to get away from the crowds.

MARK: But that didn't work?

PETER: No, they just followed us. In fact we even ended up with one of the largest crowds Jesus ever preached to. As I recall there were at least four thousand. No, I believe there were closer to five thousand people. That's right, there were five thousand men alone because Jesus had everyone sit down in groups of fifty, and there were a hundred groups of men plus all the women and children. It was impossible to count them. You know how children are. They never sit still—even at mealtime.

MARK: What do you mean mealtime? I thought they had gone to hear Jesus preach?

PETER: That's just the point, Mark. They had gone to hear Him preach, and Jesus preached so long that the people got hungry. On that side of the lake there was just no place to get food without traveling a great distance.

MARK: What did He feed them?

PETER: Well, good old Andrew came to our rescue. Even if he is my brother, he sure helped us out that day.

MARK: What did he do? He couldn't have provided the food for all of those people.

PETER: No, but he did find a young boy who had a small lunch that his mother had packed for him. He had some fish and small loaves of bread.

MARK: How many fish?

PETER: Two.

MARK: And how many loaves of bread?

PETER: Five. Mark, I wish everyone telling the story of Jesus would be as certain of the facts as you are. Let's see, where was I?

MARK: You had just said that Andrew had found a boy who had a lunch.

PETER: That's right. Well, to make a long story short, Jesus fed the people from that lunch, and then we started back across the lake.

MARK: Was that when it happened?

PETER: Yes. Jesus stayed behind. He thought that if the people saw us leave that they would think He had left too. That way He could have some time by Himself to think and pray.

MARK: So what happened then?

PETER: We got back into the boat and began to row across the lake. We had rowed about halfway across the lake. . . .

MARK: Excuse me for interrupting again, but how far was that?

PETER: We had rowed about three or four miles. We were at the widest point in the lake which is about seven miles. All the time we were rowing into a strong head wind right out of the west. Normally, it wouldn't have been a very big job. That night it was all we could do to make any progress at all. It seemed like the harder we rowed, the farther the lights on the shore got.

MARK: Were you afraid?

PETER: No, it wasn't as strong a storm as I told you about the other time. It just interfered with our rowing.

MARK: I see. Go on.

PETER: Well, I was pulling with all my strength, when I thought I caught a glimpse of something on the water. At first I thought I had just seen a cloud or a wave. But I looked closer. About that time there was a flash of lightning. There, as clear as day, we saw Jesus walking on the water a short distance from the boat. He was just walking along like He was on dry ground.

MARK: Did that alarm you?

PETER: Yes, it did. I pointed Him out to Matthew, and Matthew thought it was a ghost.

MARK: How did you find out He wasn't a ghost?

PETER: He spoke to us!

MARK: What did He say?

PETER: He said, "Don't be afraid. It is I."

MARK: How did you know it was Jesus?

MARK: There was no mistaking His voice. We had heard Him speak too many times. Only He could calm fearing hearts like that.

MARK: Did He get into the boat with you?

PETER Well, I'm rather embarrassed to tell this part. I'll tell you if you promise not to include it in your account.

MARK: All right, Peter, I promise.

PETER (*embarrassed*): I tried to walk on the water, too, and I sank.

MARK: You what!

PETER: Oh, you know how I always act first and think later. I just knew Jesus could do anything, and I asked Him to let me walk to Him.

MARK: Well, what happened? This sounds interesting.

PETER: Now remember, you are not to include this in your Gospel. You promised.

MARK: All right. But I must hear the rest of the story.

PETER: I climbed out of the boat and started walking toward Jesus.

MARK: You mean you actually walked on top of the water, just like Jesus?

PETER: Yes, at least for a few steps. Then I began to think how all the other disciples would envy me. Then I noticed the waves all around me, and then a big wave splashed over me, and I began to sink.

MARK: What did Jesus do?

PETER: Nothing. He just stood there. I thought I was going to drown. At last I cried out, "Jesus, save me. I'm drowning!" Then He reached out and took my hand and pulled me back up, and we got into the boat. It was really an embarrassing experience. The other apostles would not let me forget it. They remind me of it ever chance they get. Matthew especially enjoys ribbing me about it. The last time I saw him he mentioned it, and it happened nearly twenty-five years ago.

MARK: I'm sure that was quite an experience.

PETER: Yes, it was. I learned that when I take my eyes off Jesus and begin to let pride creep into my life that I will fall.

MARK: Good point. That will make a good story.

PETER: Now, Mark, you promised you would not mention that. You gave me your word.

MARK: Well, all right, Peter. But it really is a good story, even if it is embarrassing for you. However, you better hope for one thing.

PETER: What's that?

MARK: You better hope that Matthew never decides to write an account of Jesus' life. He'll include it for sure.

Bondage and Freedom

Scripture Reference: Luke 7:36-50
Voices: 2
Time: 4:00

SIMON: At last I've got a chance to see this Jesus up close. I've heard so much about Him. He really is a shrewd fellow. Maybe during dinner tonight I can catch Him off guard and get some evidence on Him. No one else has succeeded in trapping Him.

MARY: I know I shouldn't be here, but since Jesus forgave me of my sin that day He kept me from getting stoned, I have not been able to forget Him. I must express my love for Him somehow.

SIMON: Oh, ho! What have we here? What's Mary doing coming here tonight? I heard she had gotten religion after our plot failed to have her stoned for committing adultery. I wonder if she is going to try to embarrass me in front of my guests? I'll have one of the servants get rid of her. Hey! It looks like she's heading toward Jesus. This may be the opportunity we've been waiting for. Maybe we can get Him on a morals charge.

MARY: There He is. Jesus looks so out of place with all these Pharisees. It really makes me laugh to see Simon hosting Jesus. I thought for a moment Simon was going to have me removed, but he wouldn't dare. He knows I'd make a scene. Simon hosting Jesus! That is a joke. But, I guess he needs to hear what Jesus has to say as much as anyone else in the city of Jerusalem.

SIMON: What's Mary up to anyway? It looks like she has a bottle of perfume in her hands. This is going to be interesting.

MARY: I wonder how Jesus will react? Will He condemn me? Will He understand why I want to do this? I don't know how else to express my love for Him. I've never wanted to express my love to anyone before. If I can just pour this perfume on His feet, I will be happy.

SIMON: I never thought I'd see such brazenness—right here in my own house too! How can He just lie there and let her remove His sandals?

Oh, you might know it, here come the tears—just like a woman.
Now she is loosening her hair and wiping her tears off His feet!
Hmm. She always did have beautiful hair.

MARY: Oh, no. My tears have spotted His feet. Simon didn't even
provide a servant to wash His feet when He came in. I must wipe
them off. Everybody is looking at me. I don't care. My heart will
break inside of me if I don't show Jesus how much I love Him. Here,
in front of all these people, He won't misunderstand.

SIMON: Now she's kissing His feet! I believe we've got Him this time.
There's no way He can get out of this one. Too many people have
seen this for Him ever to live it down. We can run Him out of town
with stories about this. Good old Mary! She may be of value to us
yet. And I didn't even have to plan this one!

MARY: He hasn't moved or said anything. I've rubbed the last drop of
perfume on His feet. I must go, but I don't want to leave Him.

SIMON: This fellow must not be much of a prophet after all. All He has
to do is to take one look at Mary and he can tell what kind of a
woman she is. It looks like He's finally getting ready to say something. Let's see how He gets out of this.

MARY: He did understand! He knows exactly what I feel! I love Him so
much because He has forgiven me of so many sins.

SIMON: Now we've got Him! Who does He think He is to forgive sins?
Only God can do that. All this talk about love and forgiveness. We
can't have people running around forgiving people. People have to
pay for their sins. Now He's telling her to go in peace. Well, we'll
see how much peace He has when the whole council hears about
this. I really think we've got Him now.

MARY: Peace! That's exactly what I feel. For the first time in my life I'm
free of the gnawing feeling of guilt. I'm free! I'm free!

Perfectly Good Pigs

Scripture Reference: Based loosely on Luke 8:26-39 (Matt. 8:28-34;
Mark 5:1-20)

Voices: 3
Time: 3:45

1: Pigs! Perfectly good pigs! All drowned in the sea.

2: Several good, hardworking men put out of work in the process.

1: You've got to think of their families too. Women and children may well starve to death.

3: All right, all right. Just calm down. Tell me all about it.

1: As unbelievable as it is, the story we got was that a supposed faith healer by the name of Jesus had healed that crazy man everybody calls Mob who has roamed around the cemetery ever since his wife died.

2: He's the one that was always frightening people by jumping out and screaming at them. He scared me once. Just about gave me heart failure. I had come out to mourn all proper like when my wife's brother's cousin died. Why it's really a shame that decent people can't even attend a funeral without being harassed.

3: Well, what happened? Where does this Jesus come in? How are Mob and the pigs connected?

1: This faith healer from Galilee came over here, and Mob tried to scare Him too. But Jesus worked some spell on him and subdued him with some kind of magic.

3: Well, how did that affect the pigs?

2: Now don't rush me. I was just coming to that. Supposedly when Jesus healed Mob, He cast out the demons in him, and the demons left and entered the pigs. The pigs bolted and ran off into the sea before the herdsmen could stop them.

1: Notice he said "supposedly." Because we know that is not really possible. So many charlatans exist nowadays that one has to investigate them very carefully. Why, when I think of all the women and children who could go hungry as a result of this senseless slaughter of these perfectly good pigs, it really makes my blood boil.

3: Well, what do you think did happen then? The pigs are dead. And Mob is healed.

1: Well, we can't really be sure. But we think what happened is that there was a plot among this Healer and His disciples. You know they are all Jews. We think that His disciples saw the herd of pigs and decided that they wanted to get rid of them. So they scared them by throwing rocks at them and yelling.

3: Did anyone see them do this?

2: Well, not really. But they could have done it that way. Without any regard for the poor men who would be out of jobs.

1: And don't forget all those hungry women and children!

2: What are we going to do about it? We can't just let this kind of thing go on in our fine town. Why, no telling what could happen. If we let this kind of thing get a foothold, it could mean a decline in business for the religious shrines of all the other religions here. Some of these have been in business for years and are respected members of our community. They pay their taxes and have supported our city and our elections for years.

3: Hmm. I think you've got a point. But there is one problem. What are we going to do about Mob? We just can't let him go wandering around talking about this Jesus. Some people will believe him.

1: Oh, Mob is no problem. We can bribe him. After all, he doesn't have much money right now. If that doesn't work, we can use the old smear campaign on him. After all, several people saw him completely undressed running through the cemetery. We can laugh him out of the community. If that doesn't work, we can always let the herdsmen that he put out of work take care of him.

3: All right. But what about Jesus? Can we get rid of him?

2: I would suggest that we go as a committee of concerned citizens and ask Him to leave. We'll just tell Him to get right back in that boat of His and head back across the lake. We don't want His type around here. He's already upset the economy.

1: And don't forget the women and children. Why, some of them are probably hungry already. We must proceed with our plan immediately. I've got to go offer my condolences to the poor women and children.

Out on a Limb

Scripture Reference: Luke 19:1-10
Voices: 2
Time: 2:45

M: Jesus, I've been thinking about something.
(stops and turns to Matthew)
J: What is it, Matthew?
M: I think I have mentioned my friend, Zacchaeus, to You. You remem-

ber him, don't You? He's the one I met at the tax collector's convention in Jerusalem a couple of years ago—before I met You.

J: Oh, yes. He's the tax collector who lives here in Jericho, isn't he?

M: That's right. Well, since we are here in Jericho, I would really like for You to meet him.

J: Why, Matthew, I'd like that. I will always be grateful to you for having given that dinner for your friends right after you decided to become My disciple. That was such a great oportunity to meet some of your friends and to let them see the change that had occurred in your life. Several of them became My disciples because of that experience.

M: That's just the point. Zacchaeus needs You too. He is a very unhappy man.

J: Why do you say that?

M: Well, he's a Jew who has sold out to the Romans. I know that I was a tax collector, too, but Zacchaeus is obsessed with a hatred for his own people. He is a little, short fellow. He always has a chip on his shoulder. He has few friends. He has the unique ability of alienating everybody who would try to get close to him. No one wants to be around him.

J: Why do you want Me to meet him, then?

M: In spite of all the negative things about him, he has many good qualities.

J: Such as?

M: He is a shrewd businessman. He has made a fortune in his work. Zacchaeus has several assistants who collect the taxes for him. He stays home and counts his money. If only we could harness that kind of talent and bring it into the kingdom of God, we would have a real leader working with us.

J: He sounds like an interesting person, all right, but what makes you think he would be interested in meeting Me?

M: Because he is so lonely. He really isn't such a bad guy underneath that rough exterior. I think I can understand a little bit about how he feels. I know I wanted a friend, and You have certainly filled that void in my life. I would like for Zacchaeus to have the same opportunity to meet You.

J: Thank you, Matthew, we'll see if we can find him while we are here.

M (*turns and looks toward audience*): Look at the crowd ahead waiting

for You. We'll never find him in there. As short as he is, we could
never see him.

J: Why don't you make some inquiries about him and find out where he
lives? Maybe we could eat lunch with him.

M: That sounds like a good idea. Wait! (*excited*) There he is! (*pointing*)

J: Where?

M: Up there in the tree! He's the little guy perched on the limb.

J: Thanks, Matthew, I'll see what I can do.

Father, Forgive Them

Scripture References: Luke 23:34,43,46; John 19:26-27,28,30; Matthew
27:46; Mark 15:34

Voices: 3
Time: 3:00

FIRST READER: I hate crucifixions. They are always so messy.

SECOND READER: Yes, and they take so much time. Besides, it's hot out
here.

FIRST READER: You shouldn't complain. You were the lucky man with
the dice today. You won His robe.

SECOND READER: Look at that! That's the man who was going around
saving people! If He is really the Messiah, let Him save Himself now.

FIRST READER: Ha! Save Yourself, O king of the Jews! (*laughs*)

JESUS: "Father, forgive them; for they know not what they do."

SECOND READER: Hey, He's still alive. I wish He were already dead. I'd
like to get this over with.

FIRST READER: Look at all those women over there. I wonder what they
saw in this guy?

JESUS: "Woman, behold thy son!"

SECOND READER: He was supposed to have a whole group of followers.
I don't see but one man in the bunch. I guess what we're doing to
their leader put the fear of the gods in them.

JESUS: "Behold thy mother."

FIRST READER: Yeah, but this is such a messy business. I never have
liked it.

SECOND READER: Oh, come now, he's just a Jew. He's not even a Roman
citizen.

FIRST READER: I know, but He just doesn't look like a criminal. Have you looked into His eyes?

SECOND READER: *That's* your problem. Never look into a condemned man's eyes. The eyes will get you every time.

FIRST READER: But He's not even cursing like the other two. One filthy dog spat right in my face when I was trying to nail his arm. He made it easy for me.

JESUS: "To-day shalt thou be with me in paradise."

SECOND READER: Well, don't ever look at their eyes. By the way, we're supposed to get this over with before sundown.

FIRST READER: Yeah, it's some kind of religious holiday. These Jews have some kind of dumb law about not having criminals on the cross over a holiday.

SECOND READER: As far as I'm concerned, they have a lot of strange laws. I'll be glad when I'm through with this tour. I'll be glad to get back to Rome.

FIRST READER: I wish my tour had ended before this. I tell you, I don't like it. Something is different about this One.

SECOND READER: Well, I'll admit that when everything went dark and stayed that way for three hours that I felt a little uncomfortable too.

FIRST READER: He just seems so different. I wish I weren't involved in this One.

JESUS: "I thirst."

FIRST READER: Hey, He's thirsty. You might as well give Him a drink of that cheap wine over there. That's the least we can do for the poor fellow.

SECOND READER: Well, it will soon be over. Get that mallet that we drove the spikes with. We need to break their legs.

FIRST READER: I hate to do that. I'd rather let that dirty dog that spat in my face suffer a while.

SECOND READER: I'd like to let them all suffer. Maybe that would teach these Jews that they can't mess with Caesar.

FIRST READER: But He didn't do anything against Caesar. You heard Pilate himself say that He was innocent.

JESUS: "It is finished!"

SECOND READER: Listen! Did you hear Him cry out? It sounded like a cry of victory!

JESUS: "Father, into thy hands I commend my Spirit."

FIRST READER: He looks like He's dead.

SECOND READER: Good. We won't have to break His legs.

FIRST READER: You know, I really believe He was the Son of God.

An Unusual Thing Happened on the Road to Emmaus

Scripture References: Luke 24:13-32 (Mark 16:12-13)
Voices: 2 (Cleopas and his wife, Mary)
Time: 4:30

CLEOPAS: I'm still embarrassed to think about it.

MARY: But Cleopas, we had no real way of knowing.

CLEOPAS: I know that, Mary, but what really embarrasses me is that it took so long for us to realize who He was.

MARY: Yes, I feel bad about that too.

CLEOPAS: All along the way I had a strange feeling about Him as we walked.

MARY: It seems like it was just yesterday, but it has been a whole year now.

CLEOPAS: That hardly seems possible, but it was a year ago today that we were walking along the road out of Jerusalem on the way to Emmaus. I had cried so hard that I could hardly see the road. I really wasn't paying much attention to anything or anyone.

MARY: Nor was I. I don't even remember when I realized He was walking with us. There were other people around, and I just wasn't paying any attention to Him. I thought He was just another traveler on the road.

CLEOPAS: So did I. The first time I realized that He was walking along with us was when I said for what must have been the hundredth time, "I just can't believe all this has happened." That was when He spoke and said, "What are you two talking about? What has happened?"

MARY: My first thought was that here was someone who was from another country.

CLEOPAS: I just did not see how anyone could have been in Jerusalem and not have heard about the death of Jesus. Then I thought that maybe He was a stranger passing through the city and that He really did not know what had happened. He sounded sincere and genuinely interested in our grief.

MARY: To be honest, my first thought was that He was a spy from the Sanhedrin. We had heard rumors that they would try to infiltrate our ranks and put all of us to death just as they had done Jesus.

CLEOPAS: I thought about that, Mary, but there was just something too genuine about His manner and attitude for Him to be an informant. When He began to ask questions about what the prophets had predicted, He seemed more interested in helping rather than tricking us into admitting we were followers of Jesus.

MARY: I have wondered so many times why neither of us noticed His hands. It looks like at some point in that seven-mile-journey that we would have looked at them.

CLEOPAS: Well, we just never thought it even remotely possible that Jesus would rise from the dead. And then He was dressed differently. The robe He wore made Him look different. Who would have ever expected it? It had never been done before—except those times He raised someone. But that was even different, as Lazarus has often pointed out since.

MARY: I was amazed at the knowledge He had of the prophets. I wondered how anyone could know that much about the Writings. He sounded like He had written them.

CLEOPAS: But I still never thought that He might be Jesus.

MARY: The way He talked and explained the Scriptures made me want to listen to Him forever. As He talked, I did think about one of the sermons Jesus preached in Galilee on the mountain overlooking the lake. I had wondered if He might have been present that day and heard Jesus.

CLEOPAS: And you even asked Him if He had been on the mount that day!

MARY: Well, that wasn't any worse than when you asked Him how He knew so much about Jesus!

CLEOPAS: You're right, Mary. We were both so blind. We just never dreamed that He would come back to life.

MARY: I'm so glad you asked Him to stay with us that evening. What would have happened if we had not asked Him in?

CLEOPAS: I shudder to think what we would have missed if He had gone on.

MARY: I still didn't even think about His being Jesus as we talked while I prepared the meal.

CLEOPAS: I remember His telling you not to go to a lot of trouble. Then He mentioned a friend of His named Martha who always went to such an extent in preparing food that He really didn't enjoy it.

MARY: That should have been a clue too. What impressed me was when He invited me to sit at the table and eat with you. I should have guessed right then that He was Jesus. Only Jesus never treated women that way. He saw us as persons, not things.

CLEOPAS: I'm glad you were there too. Both of us saw Him take the bread in His hands. I know I should have done that as the host, but it seemed so natural to let Him do it. I didn't even question it.

MARY: I'll never forget His prayer. It was so direct. He talked to God like He was His father. When He finished the prayer, that's when I knew.

CLEOPAS: (*reverently*): Yes, that's when I knew too. Christ is risen!

MARY: Christ is risen, indeed!

They Have No Wine

Scripture Reference: John 2:1-10
Voices: 3
Time: 2:15

1: They have no wine.

2: Look! Mary's talking to her Son.

3: He's telling her that she must not try to tell Him what to do.

2: How embarrassing to run out of wine at a wedding feast, even here in Cana.

3: Can He really do anything about it? Does He carry extra wine around with Him? Ha!

1: They have no wine.

2: Look, He's calling the servants. They're filling the water pots with water.

3: Those are sacred water pots. They're used for religious purification rites.

2: Besides, they hold twenty to thirty gallons apiece. What's He trying to do?

1: They have no wine.

2: Listen! He's telling the servants to take the water and give it to the headwaiter.

3: Boy, is the headwaiter going to be surprised. The guests are expecting more wine and they get water!

2: He might have palmed off some cheap wine on them, but this is ridiculous.

3: What's that? Did you hear what the headwaiter said?

2: It sounded like he said that it was the best wine he had ever tasted!

3: But that's impossible. That's water. It can't be good wine. Can it?

2: There's no way that water can become wine. Is there?

3: Why, that would require a miracle.

2: Is it possible that in those old sacred purification pots that Jesus has provided something new?

3: Can He take old, meaningless religious forms and fill them with new meaning?

2: Can He really turn something so insipid as lukewarm water into sparkling wine?

3: Could He take something as commonplace as a life filled with boredom and give sparkle to it?

2: Could He take a life filled with sorrow and turn it into joy?

1: *They* have no wine.

3: Could He take my life and give me newness?

2: Could He take my old attempts at religion and give me new meaning and life?

1: *They* have no wine.

2 & 3 (*imploringly*): Lord, *we* have no wine.[1]

Note

1. *Bible Book Study for Adult Teachers: Resource Kit,* October-December, 1986. Used by permission.

He's Alive!

Scripture Reference: John 4:43-54
Voices: 3
Time: 2:45

1: He looks worried and concerned.

2: His son is quite sick.

3: Well, he really shouldn't have left Capernaum and come to Cana with his son in that shape. What would happen if his son dies?

1: He looks so sad.

2: His servant is whispering something to him.

1: I wonder if his son has died?

2: No, he looks too excited for that. Hurry! Follow him and let's see where he is going.

3: He shouldn't be going out in this hot noonday sun. The sun is straight overhead. If he is going to go out, he ought to move more slowly.

2: It looks like he's headed toward that crowd up ahead.

1: Isn't that Jesus of Nazareth?

2: Do you think he would dare ask Jesus to go all the way to Capernaum to heal his son?

3: Surely not. It's a long day's journey from Cana to Capernaum. No one would ask that of Jesus.

1: Look! Jesus appears to be upset. He must have asked Him to go to Capernaum.

2: Did you hear what Jesus said? He thinks the man is just wanting to see a miracle performed.

1: Jesus is upset with the man.

2: Could it be that Jesus is just testing the man to see if he really believes?

3: Listen, he's begging Jesus to go with him before his son dies.

2: Look at Jesus' face. He looks so kind.

3: Do you think He'll go?

1: No, Jesus is saying something to the man. What's that? I don't believe it. He told the man to go home and his son would live!

3: Well, that's one way to get rid of him. By the time he gets home, Jesus will be long gone. That's terrible to get that government man's hopes all up and then to get home and find that his son is dead. But that's the way with these faith healers.

1: I can't believe Jesus would do that.

2: I can't get away from that look in Jesus' face when he turned to help the man.

3: Well, there's no way of proving it. Even if the boy does get well, it could just be a coincidence.

1: I can't believe Jesus would get his hopes up and then disappoint him. I'm going to go with him to see.

2: So am I. No one could look like Jesus looked and be insincere.

3: He could be sincerely wrong.

1: Remember when He came to the wedding feast here in Cana and rescued the host by turning water into wine? If He was willing to help keep a man from being embarrassed by running out of wine, I believe He could heal a boy a day's journey away.

3: Even if the boy does get well, there's no way of proving that Jesus did it.

2: Who's that coming up ahead? He's seen us, and he's broken into a run.

3: It must be a messenger who has come to tell him his son has died.

1: Listen! He's shouting. He's alive! He's alive!

2: The boy was healed yesterday at noonday, at the exact time Jesus said.

1 & 2: He's alive! He's alive!

3: Lord, . . . I would like to believe too. But sometimes it's so hard. Will you help me too?

But It's the Sabbath!

Scripture Reference: John 5:1-9
Voices: 2
Time: 3:00

1: Jerusalem.

2: Jesus.

1: Bethesda.

2: Brokenness.

1: So many are sick.

2: Blind.

1: Lame.

2: Withered.

1: So much hurt gathered in one place.

2: So much hurt gathered in one place for so long.

1: Thirty-eight years.

2: Ten years.

1: Five years.

2: Yesterday.

1: Today.

2: Still they come.

1: Hoping.

2: Against hope.

1: Hoping.

2: For a miracle.

1: Listen to their cries for help.

2: Their pleas for someone to care.

1: For food.

2: For love.

1: Can't anyone do anything?

2: Someone should do something!

1: Whose heart and hands are big enough to care for all of these broken people?

2: Who could even do anything about just one of these poor, wretched souls?

1: An angel!

2: Who stirs the water!

1 (*slowly*): But what about all those who can't make it to the water? Does that mean they can never be healed?

2: What about those who have no one who cares whether they make it to the water? Does that mean they can never be loved?

1: Look! There's that man again.

2: The one they call Jesus. I was afraid He would show up here.

1: What could He be doing in a place like this?

2: He's stopping where the cripple is lying. The one who has been sick for thirty-eight years.

1: Did you hear that? Jesus asked the man if he wanted to get well!

2: Doesn't He know that everyone wants to get well?

1: Well, that would ruin his begging business.

2: He never has known any other business.

1: Maybe he would rather remain a cripple?

2: How sad, he said he had no one to put him in the healing water.

1: Will Jesus help him get into the water?

2: How cruel of Jesus to get his hopes up.

1: Do you think Jesus will heal him?

2: No one can be healed today even if the angel did stir the water. It's the sabbath.

1 (*excited*): I can't believe it! Did you hear what Jesus said?

2: Look! The man is actually getting up.

1: He's leaping and running around!

2: But he can't do that. This is the sabbath!

1: He almost fell into the pool he couldn't even get near a moment ago!

2: Boy, are our religious leaders going to be uset over this. He's even carrying his bedroll!

1: But he's whole!

2: But it's the sabbath!

1: No longer is he broken.

2: But it's the sabbath!

1: No longer does he have to beg.

2: But it's the sabbath!

1: He acts like he's just been born again.

2: Healings like this should wait until after sundown. That man wasn't going to go any place.

1: He is now! Just watch him running from person to person telling them that he has been healed.

2: But it's the sabbath!

1: It's possible that a person is more important than a law.

2: But it's the sabbath! Jesus can't just go around changing laws our fathers have established.

1: But look at the joy on the man's face.

2: Jesus has no right to change the laws. Who does He think He is?

1: God!

Guess What Jesus and I Did Today?

Scripture References: Based on John 6:1-13 (Matt. 14:13-21; Mark 6: 30-44; Luke 9:10-17)

Voices: 2

Time: 3:15

BOY (*excited*): Mother, Mother! Guess what Jesus and I did today!

MOTHER: Hey, calm down and tell me about it.

BOY: You know that I went to hear Jesus today.

MOTHER: Yes, what happened?

BOY: There were thousands and thousands of people there.

MOTHER: Now Son, are you sure there were that many people?

BOY: There were so many people that it was hard to get close to Jesus. I'm not kidding.

MOTHER: But Jesus was over on this side of the Lake of Galilee. How did all the people get here?

BOY: They followed Him around the lake. Some even sailed across the lake. But they just kept coming.

MOTHER: You mean people came all the way from Galilee to hear Him?

BOY: Yes, there were people all over the countryside. Jesus talked and talked. The people just would not let Him stop. Soon it began to get late and people began to get hungry.

MOTHER: Where could that many people get food?

BOY: That's what I have been trying to tell you. Jesus and I fed the whole crowd.

MOTHER: Son, I have tried to teach you to be truthful.

BOY: But I am telling the truth. Jesus and I fed the whole crowd.

MOTHER: I think you had better explain yourself.

BOY: I was listening to Jesus talk. I had slipped up as close as I could get to Jesus. The people seemed to listen to every word He said. Jesus talked and talked. When He finished, no one wanted to leave.

MOTHER: You still haven't told me how you and Jesus fed the crowd.

BOY: I was getting hungry so I pulled out the lunch you had packed for me this morning.

MOTHER: You mean the lunch that you didn't want to take?

BOY: Well, I didn't know I was going to be gone so long or that Jesus would want it.

MOTHER: OK. Go on.

BOY: Just as I pulled out the food, one of Jesus' disciples whose name was Andrew came up to me and asked me if I would be willing to share my lunch with Jesus. Andrew said that the crowd had kept Jesus from getting away to eat, and they were trying to find some food for Jesus.

MOTHER: Well, did you share it with Him?

BOY: Of course I did! I was more than glad to give it to Him. I told Andrew that Jesus could have all of it. I only wished that you had included some of your raisin cakes and cheese instead of just those little loaves of bread and those two dried fish.

MOTHER: Did Jesus eat your food?

BOY: Well, yes and no.

MOTHER: What do you mean? He either ate it or He didn't.

BOY: Mother, you're not going to believe what happened next. Andrew took my food to Jesus. Jesus looked over at me and smiled. Then He bowed His head and asked God to take what I had given and make it into enough for everybody.

MOTHER: What happened?

BOY: He then gave the food to the disciples, and they started passing it out. They just never seemed to run out. The more they gave, the more there was left. Jesus even let me help pass out the food. Andrew said there were more than five thousand people who were fed.

MOTHER: You mean there was enough in that lunch that I packed for you this morning to feed five thousand people?

BOY: Not only that, when everyone had eaten we went around and picked up all that was left and there were twelve basketsful of fish and bread left.

MOTHER: Now, Son, I have told you not to exagerate and stretch the truth.

BOY: But mother, that is exactly what happened! Jesus and I fed the whole crowd!

MOTHER: Son, I can't believe you would go hear a man like Jesus and then come home and tell a tall tale like this. You know things like this don't happen. Only God could perform that kind of miracle.

BOY (*reverently*): I know, Mother, I know.

A Life Worthy of Your Calling

Scripture Reference: Ephesians 4:1 to 5:1 (GNB and KJV)
Voices: 5
Time: 2:15

NARRATOR: "I . . . beseech you that ye walk worthy of the vocation wherewith you are called."

FIRST READER: But who can determine if we are doing that? I'm not even sure what that means.

SECOND READER: Surely we're not supposed to be perfect . . . are we?

NARRATOR: "I . . . beseech you that ye walk worthy of the vocation wherewith you are called."

FIRST READER: Well, what does that really mean?

SECOND READER: Can you tell me how?

FIRST VOICE: "Be always humble, gentle, and patient."

SECOND VOICE: "Show your love by being tolerant with one another."

FIRST VOICE: "Do your best to preserve the unity which the Spirit gives."

SECOND VOICE: "Each one of us has received a special gift in proportion to what Christ has given."

FIRST VOICE: Christ has "appointed some to be apostles, others to be prophets, others to be evangelists, others to be pastors and teachers."

NARRATOR: "I . . . beseech you that ye walk worthy of the vocation wherewith you are called."

FIRST READER: I'm beginning to understand.

SECOND READER: Can you tell us more?

FIRST VOICE: "We shall become mature people reaching to the very height of Christ's full stature."

SECOND VOICE: "We shall no longer be children, carried by the waves and blown about by every shifting wind of the teaching of deceitful men."

FIRST VOICE: "By speaking the truth in a spirit of love, we must grow up in every way to Christ, who is the head."

SECOND VOICE: "When each separate part works as it should, the whole body grows and builds itself up through love."

NARRATOR: "I . . . beseech you that ye walk worthy of the vocation wherewith you are called."

FIRST READER: So that's what it means.

SECOND READER: I never knew so much was involved. Is there more?

FIRST VOICE: "Do not continue to live like the heathen, whose thoughts are worthless and whose minds are in the dark."

SECOND VOICE: "Get rid of your old self."

FIRST VOICE: "Your hearts and minds must be made completely new."

SECOND VOICE: "You must put on the new self."

FIRST VOICE: "No more lying."

SECOND VOICE: "Do not stay angry all day."

FIRST VOICE: "Do not use harmful words, but only helpful words, the kind that build up."

SECOND VOICE: "Do not make God's Holy Spirit sad."

FIRST VOICE: "Get rid of all bitterness, passion, and anger."

SECOND VOICE: "No more hateful feelings of any sort."

FIRST VOICE: "Be kind and tender-hearted to one another."

SECOND VOICE: "Forgive one another, as God has forgiven you through Christ."

FIRST READER: But all this sounds so difficult.

SECOND READER: It sounds almost like we're supposed to be as good as God.

NARRATOR: "I . . . beseech you that ye walk worthy of the vocation wherewith ye are called." "Since you are God's dear children, you must try to be like him."

4

Biblical Readings

Biblical readings need special consideration. We are most familiar with either a single person reading the Scripture or with using responsive readings in a worship service. Both of these are valid ways of publicly reading God's Word. However, they need not be the only ways His Word is read aloud.

A biblical reading is similar to a choral reading except it is a presentation of the biblical text. The text is a given; how the text is presented is open to interpretation.

Ancient Israel read the Scriptures aloud and at least on some occasions they tried to vary the method. Psalm 136 is one of these "experiments" with a different form of reading. Consider the following: "O give thanks unto the Lord for he is good: . . . O give thanks unto the God of gods: . . . O give thanks to the Lord of Lords: . . . To him who alone doeth great wonders: . . . To him that by wisdom made the heavens" (vv. 1-5).

This is the way the text reads—almost! If you are familiar with the psalm, you immediately recognize that I have left something out: a refrain. After each phrase the psalmist added the refrain: "for his mercy endureth for ever." Apparently the priest read the statement about God, and the people responded with the refrain: "for his mercy endureth for ever."

> PRIEST: "O give thanks unto the Lord; for he is good:
> PEOPLE: "for his mercy endureth for ever.
> PRIEST: "O give thanks unto the God of gods:
> PEOPLE: "for his mercy endureth for ever.
> PRIEST: "O give thanks to the Lord of lords:
> PEOPLE: "for his mercy endureth for ever.
> PRIEST: "To him who alone doeth great wonders:

PEOPLE: "For his mercy endureth for ever."

Doesn't that read much better? Many of the psalms were intended for this type of antiphonal reading. Even the law was read in this manner. The Lord told Moses to "place the blessing on Mount Gerizim and the curse on Mount Ebal" (Deut. 11:29, NASB). Later Moses was more specific: "When you cross the Jordan, these shall stand on Mount Gerizim to bless the people: Simeon, Levi, Judah, Issachar, Joseph, and Benjamin. And for the curse, these shall stand on Mount Ebal: Reuben, Gad, Asher, Zebulun, Dan, and Naphtali" (Deut. 27:12-13, NASB). Then follows twelve "curses" that the Israelites take upon themselves if they violate the law. After each curse the people were instructed to reply: "Amen" (Deut. 27:15).

In a time when people did not all have copies of the Scriptures, leaders of worship sought to provide ways for the people to remember and participate in the reading of the Scripture. Several of the psalms are acrostics. Each verse begins with a consecutive letter of the Hebrew alphabet. The most famous of these acrostics is Psalm 119. These early worship leaders recognized the need to make vivid the reading of God's Word so the people would remember it.

Today we face a different problem, but the end result is the same. We have heard the Word read so much that we do not alway pay attention to it when it is read. So we "hear" but then we do not hear. The Word does not find a place in our hearts.

Biblical readings can help people understand and remember God's Word. They can "hear" it. Some passages in the Bible are already written to be used in this manner with one person reading a phrase and another person or group responding. However, other passages can have a refrain added. Psalm 33:1-5 is an example.

LEADER: "Sing for joy in the Lord, O you righteous ones;"
PEOPLE: For his mercy endureth forever.
LEADER: "Praise is becoming to the upright."
PEOPLE: For his mercy endureth forever.
LEADER: "Give thanks to the Lord with the lyre;"
PEOPLE: For his mercy endureth forever.
LEADER: "Sing praises to Him with a harp of ten strings;"
PEOPLE: For his mercy endureth forever.
LEADER: "Sing to Him a new song;"

PEOPLE: For his mercy endureth forever.
LEADER: "Play skillfully with a shout of joy."
PEOPLE: For his mercy endureth forever.
LEADER: "For the word of the Lord is upright;"
PEOPLE: For his mercy endureth forever.
LEADER: "And all His work is done in faithfulness."
PEOPLE: For his mercy endureth forever.
LEADER: "He loves righteousness and justice;"
PEOPLE: For his mercy endureth forever.
LEADER: "The earth is full of the lovingkindness of the Lord"
(NASB).
PEOPLE: For his mercy endureth forever.

This reading could be presented by two people; one person reading each part. Or it could be presented by one person reading the leader's part and a class or group responding. Instead of a class or group, it would be possible to use this in a worship service, using the pastor as the leader and the choir to repeat the refrain.

This type of biblical reading is fairly easy to construct. How about something more difficult?

Any passage can be used, even Old Testament narrative passages. (See biblical reading on Jer. 11:1-8.)

Passages of Scripture that adapt to biblical readings best are those that have several speaking parts and a narrator as well. The reading on Matthew 2:1-12 breaks down easily into seven voices: a narrator, three Wise Men, chief priests, a prophet, and Herod. If you wished to use more voices, you could assign several voices to the chief priests and more than three voices to the Wise Men.

You may want to use different translations for different readings. The birth narrative is familiar enough that most people understand it. Some Old Testament passages may be more understandable if you use a modern translation. Another distinct advantage of modern translations that use quotation marks is that it will help you break down the reading into appropriate voices. Even if you choose to use the King James Version, the modern translations will help you know who is speaking and when a speaker changes.

The reading on Jeremiah 11:1-8 (with modification) suggests how you can slightly modify the form without changing the meaning. I wanted to emphasize that what Jeremiah prophesied was God's Wod, so I used the refrain throughout the reading: "The Word of the Lord came to Jeremiah." In most of the places where this refrain appears some other statement is printed in the Bible that means basically the same thing. By using the repetition of the refrain, I felt I could communicate the message even stronger.

If you teach a class or a Bible study, you read the Scriptures aloud regularly. The extra time spent in preparing a biblical reading would add much to your teaching. Experiment with this approach and watch God's Word come alive to your group.

Biblical Reading

Scripture Reference: Jeremiah 11:1-8 (with modification)
Voices: 4
Time: 1:30

1: The word of the Lord came to Jeremiah:
2: "Hear ye the words of this covenant,
3: "and speak unto the men of Judah,
4: "and to the inhabitants of Jerusalem; . . ."
1: The word of the Lord came to Jeremiah:
2: "Cursed be the man that obeyeth not the words of his covenant,
3: "Which I commanded your fathers in the day that I brought them forth out of the land of Egypt,
4: "from the iron furnace."
1: The word of the Lord came to Jeremiah:
2: "Obey my voice,
3: "and do . . . all which I command you:
4: "so shall ye be my people,
2: "and I will be your God:
3: "That I may perform the oath which I have sworn unto your fathers,
4: "to give them a land flowing with milk and honey,
3: "as it is this day."
1: The word of the Lord came to Jeremiah:
2: "Hear ye the words of this covenant,
3: "and do them.

4: "For I earnestly protested unto your fathers in the day that I brought them up out of the land of Egypt,

2: "even unto this day,

3: "rising early and protesting."

1: The word of the Lord came to Jeremiah:

2: "Obey my voice.

3: "Yet they obeyed not,

4: "nor inclined their ear,

2: "but walked everyone in the imagination of their evil heart."

1: The word of the Lord came to Jeremiah:

2: "therefore I will bring upon them all the words of this covenant,

3: "which I commanded them to do;

4: "but they did them not."

1: This is the word of the Lord to Jeremiah.

Biblical Reading

Scripture Reference: Hosea 1:1-8; 3:1-5 (GNB)
Voices: 4
Time: 2:15

1: "This is the message which the Lord gave Hosea son of Beeri during the time that Uzziah, Jotham, Ahaz, and Hezekiah were kings of Judah, and Jeroboam son of Jehoash was king of Israel.

2: "When the Lord first spoke to Israel through Hosea, he said to Hosea,

3: " 'Go and get married; your wife will be unfaithful, and your children will be just like her. In the same way my people have left me and become unfaithful.'

1: "So Hosea married a woman named Gomer, the daughter of Diblaim. After the birth of their first child, a son, the Lord said to Hosea,

3: " 'Name him "Jezreel," because it will not be long before I punish the king of Israel for the murders that his ancestor Jehu committed at Jezreel. I am going to put an end to Jehu's dynasty. And in Jezreel Valley I will at that time destroy Israel's military power.'

2: "Gomer had a second child—this time it was a girl. The Lord said to Hosea,

3: " 'Name her "Unloved," because I will no longer show love to the people of Israel or forgive them. But to the people of Judah I will show love. I, the Lord their God, will save them, but I will not do it by war—with swords or bows and arrows or with horses and horsemen.'

1: "After Gomer had weaned her daughter, she became pregnant again and had another son. The Lord said to Hosea,

3: " 'Name him "Not-My-People," because the people of Israel are not my people, and I am not their God.'

2: "The Lord said to me,

3: " 'Go again and show your love for a woman who is committing adultery with a lover. You must love her just as I still love the people of Israel, even though, they turn to other gods and like to take offerings of raisins to idols.'

4: "So I paid fifteen pieces of silver and seven bushels of barley to buy her. I told her that for a long time she would have to wait for me without being a prostitute or committing adultery; and during this time I would wait for her.

1: "In just this way the people of Israel will have to live a long time without kings or leaders,

2: "without sacrifices or sacred stone pillars,

4: "without idols or images to use for divination.

2: "But the time will come when the people of Israel will once again turn to the Lord their God. . . .

4: "Then they will fear the Lord and will receive his good gifts."

Biblical Reading

Scripture Reference: Matthew 2:1-12
Voices: 7
Time: 1:30

NARRATOR: "Now when Jesus was born in Bethlehem of Judaea in the days of Herod the king, behold, there came wise men from the east to Jerusalem, Saying,

THREE WISE MEN: "Where is he that is born King of the Jews? for we have seen his star in the east, and are come to worship him.

NARRATOR: "When Herod the king had heard these things, he was troubled, and all Jerusalem with him. And when he had gathered

all the chief priests and scribes of the people together, he demanded
of them where Christ should be born. And they said unto him,

CHIEF PRIESTS: "Bethlehem of Judaea: for thus it is written by the
prophet,

PROPHET: "And thou Bethlehem, in the land of Juda, art not the least
among the princes of Juda: for out of thee shall come a Governor,
that shall rule my people Israel.

NARRATOR: "Then Herod, when he had privily called the wise men,
inquired of them diligently what time the star appeared. And he sent
them to Bethlehem, and said,

HEROD: "Go and search diligently for the young child; and when ye have
found him, bring me word again, that I may come and worship him
also.

NARRATOR: "When they had heard the king, they departed: and, lo, the
star, which they saw in the east, went before them, till it came and
stood over where the young child was. When they saw the star, they
rejoiced with exceeding great joy. And when they were come into
the house, they saw the young child with Mary his mother, and fell
down, and worshipped him: and when they had opened their trea-
sures, they presented unto him gifts:

FIRST WISE MAN: "gold,

SECOND WISE MAN: "and frankincense,

THIRD WISE MAN: "and myrrh.

NARRATOR: "And being warned of God in a dream that they should not
return to Herod, they departed into their own country another
way."

Biblical Reading

Scripture Reference: Luke 14:7-14 (GNB)
Voices: 3
Time: 2:00

NARRATOR: "Jesus noticed how some of the guests were choosing the
best places, so he told this parable to all of them:

JESUS: "When someone invites you to a wedding feast, do not sit down
in the best place. It could happen that someone more important

than you has been invited, and your host, who invited both of you, would have to come and say to you,

HOST: " 'Let him have this place.'

JESUS: "Then you would be embarrassed and have to sit in the lowest place. Instead, when you are invited, go and sit in the lowest place, so that your host will come to you and say,

HOST: " 'Come on up, my friend, to a better place.'

JESUS: "This will bring you honor in the presence of all the other guests. For everyone who makes himself great will be humbled, and everyone who humbles himself will be made great.' "

NARRATOR: "Then Jesus said to his host,

JESUS: "When you give a lunch or a dinner, do not invite your friends or your brothers or your relatives or your rich neighbors—for they will invite you back, and in this way you will be paid for what you did. When you give a feast, invite the poor, the crippled, the lame, and the blind; and you will be blessed, because they are not able to pay you back. God will repay you on the day the good people rise from death."

5

Monologues

Monologues fit into a category by themselves. They need only one person to present them. If done poorly they can be extremely boring; if done well, they can be quite effective. Monologues require a creative imagination to keep them believable and, at the same time, interesting. Yet, they can be one of the most effective ways of presenting biblical truth.

Monologues are simply a retelling of a particular event from one person's point of view. This can be both good and bad. It can be bad because the Bible seldom gives us the personal feelings of individuals about particular situations. It can be good because this allows you to try to think like a biblical character. Few things will help you get inside the skin of a biblical character as much as a monologue. Granted, we seldom have enough information to know all about a particular person, but we do have enough that we can pick up on certain feelings and reactions that biblical characters *could* have had.

A monologue enables you to place yourself in the position of the biblical character. For example, "Peter by the Fire" expresses many of my own bungling attempts in living the Christian life. All of the reasons Peter gives could have been his, but they definitely are mine. Yet, Peter does not come out as being an unbelievable character. There is a universality in our failure to commit our lives to Christ and then attempt to explain away our lack of commitment.

Monologues allow you to experience the feelings of the biblical characters. If you had been in this person's place, what would you have felt? Another way of understanding a character's feelings is to ask yourself, if this person had kept a diary, what would have been written about this event?

Monologues give you a lot of opportunity to use your creative imagination. You can also use monologues to express feelings and reactions that people today have and put them in the lives of biblical characters.

Monologues allow you to express feelings of confession and repentance and to call for a similar response from your audience.

If you are going to write your own monologues, consider the following points:

- Select a biblical character that most people will have some knowledge of. This will keep you from having to explain a lot of information about the character. This does not necessarily mean that people must know the character's name and all the information about him. For example, "A Funny Thing Happened on the Way to Jericho" utilizes a priest whose name we do not even know. Yet, most people know that a priest was involved in the parable of the good Samaritan.

- Keep the monologue believable. Be certain that all you have your characters say *could* have been said by them. It is hard for people to separate fact from fiction in monologues. If you do include information that is not biblical, be sure it is obvious.

- You can use humor as a way of making a point. For example, in "A Funny Thing Happened on the Road to Jericho" the fact that there were no Southern Jewish Convention and no Jewish Life Centers in the first century can serve as a source of humor. No one would think that these organizations actually existed. However, the fact that we have these conventions and Christian life centers today allows us to create smiles when they are superimposed on a first-century Jewish rabbi. We can laugh at ourselves for the emphasis we give them.

- Monologues can be a good way to communicate particular ideas about modern topics. However, be careful not to preach at your audience. Let the message flow naturally rather than letting it become artificial.

- Monologues do not have to be long. In fact they can be quite brief. What matters is that you communicate your message.

Peter by the Fire

Scripture Reference: Matthew 26:69-75 (Mark 14:66-72; Luke 22:56-62; John 18:15,18,25-27)

Voices: 1
Time: 2:00

Deny Him? Of course I wouldn't deny Him! I have to admit that to a casual bystander that it might look like I denied him, but *deny* is a little too strong of a word. Let me tell you why I did what I did.

Don't forget that I am one of only two disciples who even followed Jesus into this courtyard tonight. Now didn't that take courage? I'll have you know it did! Why, this is a dangerous place to be tonight. Anything could happen here with this ugly mob. Why, a man could lose his life around this bloodthirsty crew. What I did was really a very wise and courageous thing.

I didn't deny Jesus. Not really. It may sound like that, but there are extenuating circumstances. As far as the actual *words,* I guess they sound pretty bad. That is, when you take them out of context. But I didn't mean them in the way some may have taken them. After all, we must use a little common sense in witnessing for our faith. Just suppose I had come right out and admitted I was one of His disciples. What do you think would have happened to me? Why, there would be four crosses on Golgotha tomorrow instead of three. And what good would that do? Really, now, what good would that do? Would it have helped anyone? Would it save Jesus? Would it have helped the faith? Who would guide the church in these difficult days ahead? Why the church needs my skills and leadership. So, what looks so calloused on the outside was really a mark of shrewd maneuvering on my part. My act just probably saved the church.

And those curses. I really didn't mean them. I was just trying to convince the soldiers around that fire that I was a real he-man. Some people think that this Christianity business is only for weak-kneed cowards. But I'll have you know that it is for real men. Do you see my ploy? When all those men around the fire heard me, I'm sure I won their respect. They are so used to hearing profanity in their line of work, and I'm sure they appreciated hearing it from me. I really communicated with them. And that's the name of the game. Communication.

Later, I'll go back and witness to them. After all, you have to earn people's respect before you can share your faith with them. I was just trying to catch them off guard, to slip up on their blind side.

So you see, everything is not just as it seems on the surface. What looks like a downright denial was really a piece of crafty footwork that kept the church from getting wiped out and destroyed. I really think the Master will be proud of me. I haven't done anything wrong. I'm here by Him so I can support Him in His time of need, and I have helped preserve the future leadership of the church. That's really quite a feat. Don't you agree?

Wait! Here He comes now. I'll stand over here by myself so He can see me. It still isn't quite safe to identify too closely with Him. I won't have to wave or indicate that I know Him. He'll understand. He'll know why I did what I did.

He's getting closer. Oh! He looks terrible! I didn't realize. . . . Those thorns on His head! His back is a bloody mass. He's turning His head this way. I think He sees me now. Yes, He's looking right . . . at . . . me. I can see . . . His eyes.

Excuse . . . me . . . please. My eye . . . seems . . . to have gotten . . . something . . . in . . . it.

A Funny Thing Happened on the Way to Jericho

Scripture Reference: Loosely based on Luke 10:25-37
Voices: 1
Time: 7:30

What's that? Who said that? I don't see anybody around here? Huh? Naw, it couldn't be, . . . could it? Things like this don't happen, do they? Is it really You, Lord? I mean, after all, I really didn't think You'd ever come to see me. What's the purpose of this visit? (*listens*) Oh, sure, I know You're in charge. You just have my curiosity aroused, that's all. You've got to admit that it's not every day that You come to visit a priest. Most of the time You visited only prophets. And the great ones at that. (*listens*) Oh, I see. It was Your visit that made them great. I'd just never thought of it that way before. But it does make sense.

Well, all right Lord. I'm waiting for You to tell me what's on your mind. S-a-y. Wait a minute! Things seem different. What's happening here? It's almost as though I had di. . . . No, it couldn't be. That's not the way we were taught in rabbinical school. Death's not supposed to be like this. It's . . . supposed . . . to be . . . different.

I see. We were wrong? But how was I to know. All of my collegues believed the same way I believed. We couldn't all be wrong, could we?

Well, I can't wait to see their faces. Especially old Eleazer's! He was always so cer. . . . What's that? This is a serious time, and not a time for making fun of my colleagues? Sorry. Let's get on with this judgment.

I really don't have a lot to be afraid of. I was a priest for fifty-three years. My father was a priest, and his father was a priest, and his father. (*hesitates*) What do You mean that doesn't count for anything? All those years of service in the Temple have to count for something! Don't they? Well, I had always counted on that. Let's see, then, I *am* a child of the covenant, born of the tribe of Levi, circumcised on the eigh. . . . Come on now, don't tell me that's not going to do me any good! What's the use of being born of good blood if it doesn't get you into heaven? You say there's another reason? Hmm. Priesthood. Lineage. What else could it be? (*thinks*) (*excited*) Of course! How foolish of me! I had just forgotten. But I'm all right on that account, too. I was the largest contributor in our synagogue. I gave more money than anyone else to our building program for the new Jewish Life Center. I also was the largest tither in our whole synagogue association, and our association led the whole Southern Jewish Convention in giving. I even tithed the plants out of my garden. It was really hard to count all the leaves on my mint plants and pinch off every tenth one. But the really hard job was to count all the dill seeds and be sure I didn't give too, . . . I mean, that I gave enough. Yes, sir. Nobody out-tithed me!

What's that? That wasn't what You had in mind either? But Lord, what's left? (*listens*) Re-la-tion-ships? Oh, You mean how I treated my relations? Do mother-in-laws count? Well, that brother-in-law of mine had it coming.

That's still not quite what you meant? What could You mean? (*listens*) With Sa . . . Sa . . . Samar . . . i . . . tans? Well, if that's all, then I'm home free. I never had anything to do with those lousy half-bre. . . . (*relieved*) I thought this judgment thing was going to be rather difficult. I feel a lot better. I never had a thing to do with them so You can't fault me there. I never associated with one of them. I never ate with one of them. I only saw them at a distance.

What? Jericho Road? I don't remember any Samaritan on the Jericho Road? Leading a donkey? On his way to Jerusalem when I was going to Jericho? (*thinks*) Oh, yeah, I remember. But I didn't do anything to him. I even warned him about the danger of robbers.

What's that? I'm getting close? (*slightly embarrassed, but pleased*) Oh, now I know what You're talking about. That was such a minor thing, too. I didn't think even You would have noticed that. You must be talking about my efforts to organize the "Rid the Road of Robbers" campaign that I initiated after that trip when I saw that Samaritan. Well, it really wasn't anything at all.

I'm right? It wasn't anything? But . . . but . . . Who? When? (*listens*) No, I don't remember seeing anyone in need that day. (*Listens*) A Jew lying in a ditch? Oh, you mean the one who had his head bashed in and all his clothes stolen who was lying on his right side by the big rock in that dry ravine that ran beside the road. No, I didn't see him. I don't remember him at all. You must have me mistaken with some other priest. You know there are more than twenty thousand of us priests. And, you know how it is, all we priests look alike.

You're certain? It really was me that day? But how could I have seen him? I was clear over on the other side of the road from where he was lying in that pool of blood. Why, I couldn't possibly have heard him groaning and gasping for water and crying out for help. I was too far away to hear or to see.

Relationships? Well, Lord, I just don't see how you can find me guilty on that account. I most solemnly swear that I did not have anything to do with that poor sucker. I don't associate with people who go around getting their heads bashed in.

Need me? Aw, not really. He was just one of those common people. (*listens*) How do I know? Well, you could tell from a great distance by the way he was dressed. (*listens*) Oh, yes, that's right. He didn't have any clothes on, did he? Well, I'm sure if he had, I would have been right. You wouldn't have expected me to go around associating with them, would You? Let me ask You a question. Now tell me honestly. Would You really want to associate with them? (*listens*) Your *who* did? I didn't even know You had a Son. Jesus? Jesus. That name sounds familiar, but so many quacks showed up all the time telling us they were the Messiah that a fellow just didn't know who to believe. I couldn't follow after all of them.

You only wanted me to follow after One of them? But how was I to know which one? There You go using the word again, *relationships.* How could I ever have guessed that Your Son would have even wanted to be associated with someone so common who never entered the Temple, who never tithed, or did anything else religious? Why would He have had the slightest interest in them with so many of us religious people around?

You *loved* them? Why? What did they ever do to earn your love? Just because you created them? Hmm. I had never thought of it that way before. You mean You created the common people as well as us priests? I had noticed a few similarities, but I thought that was just coincidental. But did you *really* love them? (*listens*) You . . . loved . . . them as much as you . . . loved me? You let Your Son die for them? I didn't know that, God. I'm sorry. Forgive me. (*bows head in silence*)

The Prodigal Son

Scripture Reference: Luke 15:11-32
Voices: 1
Time: 3:00

I have really messed up my life. I can't believe I'm here in this strange country slopping hogs. I thought I was going to be so free. I had gotten tired of having to obey all the rules at home. I just had to get away and try things my way. But I didn't think it would turn out like this. I thought it would be fun.

I guess it was fun for a while. Sort of. All the parties and friends. It was great to be the center of attention. I got invited to everything. With all of the money father gave me I didn't have to work, so I could do anything I wanted. It felt good to be recognized and spoken to when I came into a room. I really felt like somebody.

But I'm not anybody now. Here I am in this stinking pigpen without any friends whatsoever. And I thought all those people were my friends! They sure took off when my money ran out.

No friends. No food. No father. Father! I wonder what he is doing? I never realized how much a part of me he really is until now. Even the money I spent here was really his money. He didn't have to give it to me. What I can't understand is why he didn't stop me. If he had said no I wouldn't be in this mess. It's all his fault.

(*Pause*) No, that's not fair. I don't have anyone to blame but myself. I can never forget the look of hurt and pain on his face as I left that morning. I guess he could see what was ahead of me and knew how much I had to learn. I thought he was upset because I wouldn't obey him and stay around and live in his house.

Oh, well, it's too late for that kind of thinking. But I do wish I had never left. I don't know what I'm going to do to keep from starving to death. I may have to sell myself as a slave. A slave! Who would have thought I would be a slave. I never gave the servants back home a second thought. I just thought they were there to wait on me. Life does some strange things. I used to own servants, and now I'm in worse shape than they are. I'd trade places with any one of the servants at home. I'd love to get old Benjamin's job. He doesn't do anything, anyway.

Hmmmm. Naw, I couldn't do that. I can't go back. That would be too embarrassing. But I'm hungry. Which is worse: to swallow my pride and eat or to keep my pride and starve? That's really not much of a choice. But Father would never take me back, anyway. And Reuben would never let me hear the last of it. Older brothers are such a pain. He was one of the reasons I left in the first place.

But I'm hungry. Even the slop I'm feeding these hogs is beginning to look good. I've got to do something. I know father hires workers to help in the harvest. Surely he would give me a job as a hired hand. I really don't have much to lose. I guess I can starve to death there as well as here if he won't hire me. Anyway, I've got to tell him how sorry I am for all the hurt I've cause him even if he won't forgive me. Maybe he'll at least give me a job working as a servant. I won't even ask to be his son; if he will just give me any job that will be enough for me.

Sooey, pig! Get out of here! I'm going home!

The Waiting Father

Scripture Reference: Luke 15:11-32
Voices: 1
Time: 2:45

How long has he been gone? A year? Two years? Time just seems to run together. It seems like it was only yesterday that he walked down this road and disappeared in the distance. On the other hand, it seems like he's been gone a lifetime. I thought my heart would break when he left. The morning when he asked to have his share of the family fortune so he could get out from under my influence and be on his own was the saddest day of my life.

He is so young. But he would not have listened to me or anyone else. He had to learn for himself. How I wish he would have listened to me. I could have saved him so much hurt. Why do children have to rebel?

I wonder where he is? We've had no word from him. Only those stories that came from the traders who said they saw him in Decapolis. It's hard to believe he even left Judea. I wonder if he is still alive? Surely he could not have grown up in our house and not have some love for us? At least I would have thought that he would care enough to send a message to let us know that he is still alive. But maybe he isn't? Maybe he's sick someplace and needs me?

I keep hoping that some day he'll come back. I can't count the number of times I have looked down this road and thought I saw him coming. But it's always someone else. Or nothing else. I guess my imagination is even beginning to play tricks on me. I want him to come home so much that I begin to see him coming down the road. But he never comes.

Reuben says good riddance. I wish those two could have gotten along. I know brothers fight, but those two were always at each other's throats. Reuben has shown no sympathy since he left, but is still as unbending as ever. I love both my sons, but I can't live their lives for them.

What! I guess my old eyes are playing tricks on me again. For a moment it looked like someone coming down the road. But even if it were someone, it wouldn't be him. Someone . . . is coming! Is . . . it . . . possible that it might be . . . him? It does sort of look like him. He has his same familiar walk. Can it possibly be? Has he come home? It is him! He has come home! My son! My son! My son!

The Elder Brother

Scripture Reference: Luke 15:11-32
Voices: 1
Time: 3:00

I can't believe it! I just can't believe it! Listen to all that noise going on inside. A regular party. All because that worthless scum has come home. I don't know why father should be so happy over it. I don't ever want to see that scoundrel again. He is no longer any brother of mine.

When he walked out of the house with his share of the fortune as far as I'm concerned he walked out of my life.

I wish he'd stayed gone. But that's just like him. He always did know how to milk the old man for all he's worth. Father is so stupid. Can't he see what that rascal has done? He's spent all his money, disgraced the family name, humiliated himself, and now he comes crawling back asking for forgiveness. I'll never forgive him. Never! I'll make him suffer until the day I die! What right does he have to be forgiven? He's wasted his money on all those parties and prostitutes. Why should I forgive him? He's had all the fun while I've stayed here and had to work. Does he think he can just say he's sorry and expect to have the slate wiped clean? If that were possible, where would that lead? People all over everywhere would be sinning and then saying they were sorry. He has to pay for his sins. He must learn that forgiveness is not that easy.

Father just does not understand how I feel. I can't believe he came out here and wanted me to come in to the party. And his attempt to buy me off by saying that all he had is mine just won't wash, either. Fat chance of that now! That scoundrel son of his took his part of the fortune and spent it. Now he's back and Father will feed him, clothe him, and treat him just like he did before he left. And all of that out of my share of the family fortune! Because he came back, there's less for me. I just can't buy that bit about his son being lost and now being found. What about me? I've given him a lifetime of obedience, and this is how he repays me. I would like to have gone away, too, but did I do it? No siree. I stayed here and took care of the farm. I broke my back while his other son was out hustling prostitutes. Little thanks I got for that. Father's never given me a party. Not once. He hasn't even killed me a goat, much less that young calf he had been fattening in the pen.

Forgive him? Never! I'll never forgive either one of them! I'd rather see them both in their graves than forgive them.

A Woman of Jerusalem

Scripture Reference: John 8:1-11
Voices: 1
Time: 4:15

Who does He think He is? What makes Him think He has any right

to pass judgment on me? I hate that man! I hate all men! If it weren't
for a man who professed love for me, I wouldn't be here now. Where is
that sniveling coward, Eleazar, anyway? He said he loved me. Let him
prove it now by stepping forward. Wait! There he is! It looks like they've
arrested him, too. He's talking to one of the Pharisees. Now they're
pointing this way, and they're both laughing!

Why am I so stupid? I've been set up! This was all planned. I am just
a thing to be used to accomplish their purpose. Why was I so blind? Look
at them. They all look so sanctimonious in their long robes. If anybody
would listen I could give them the names of a few others in this crowd
who ought to be here with me. There's Simon, Eli, and, of course,
Eleazar. But nobody would even suspect these leaders of the Jews.

Who is this Jesus anyway? I wonder why they want to trap Him? Why
should they bring me to Him? What right does He have to pass judgment
on me? Is He God? Did He make the rules?

I've heard a lot of crazy stories about Him. He's the one who cleaned
house at the Temple recently. Then there was some story about His
turning water into wine. I think He was supposed to have healed a lot
of people, too.

But does that make Him an authority over me? I hate Him! I hate all
men! They're all traitors. Every man I've ever known would sell his own
mother if he could profit by it.

Well, at last that old windbag, Eli, has finished laying out my sin. I
wonder why he didn't tell about our meeting last week! As if I didn't
know the answer! I'll be stoned, and he and all the rest will go on their
merry way. They'll just find some other woman.

I wonder if it will hurt much? I hope the first rock is hard enough to
knock me out. I don't want to die! I want to live! It's not fair. I wasn't
the only one involved.

Hey! What's going on here? This Jesus fellow isn't saying anything.
He's stooped down and is writing with His finger in the dust. It looks
like He's writing a bunch of names. S-i-m-o-n. E-l-i. E-l-e-a-z-a-r. How
did Jesus know? He's looking straight at Eli. Ha! The sinner blushes!
What's that? Let the one among you who has never sinned throw the first
stone. Hey! I like that! Look at Eli! He's backing away. There goes
Simon. And Eleazar is right behind him! The whole crowd is breaking
up. Maybe I'm going to get out of this with my life after all.

What's Jesus writing in the dust now? M-a-r-y. Hey! That's my name!

He knows about me. Well, I guess I'll get a sermon now on how to be a good girl.

I wish He'd look at me. Why doesn't He go ahead and get it over with? He just keeps staring at the dust. Oh, I guess my robe is ripped quite a bit. He really is a gentleman. Somehow He does seem different from any other man I've ever met. Just standing here in His presence I feel so dirty and unclean. Just by the way He sits there staring at the dust, I get the feeling that He respects me. I've never felt that from any man. Oh, how I wish my past could be taken away, and I could begin life new and fresh.

What? Oh, no, Sir. They have all gone. No one has accused me. . . . My Lord, you know I'm guilty. You've written my name in the dust along with the others. I'm sorry for my sin. . . . Forgive me? Can you really? But I don't deserve. . . . Oh, thank You! Thank You! I've heard the word all my life, but You have shown me what love really is.

And It Was Night

Scripture Reference: John 13:1-30 (Matt. 26:20-25; Mark 14:17-21; Luke 22:21-23)

Voices: 1
Time: 5:45

Oh no, what's He doing now? He's always up to something. I wonder if He knows? Surely not, for the high priest agreed to keep our bargain a secret. And the thirty pieces of silver—even if He sees them He'll just think they're a part of the treasury.

I can't believe it! He has taken off His robe and wrapped a towel around His waist. Now He's picking up a pitcher of water and a bowl. I wish somebody would ask Him what He's up to. He's headed toward John. Now He's stooping down and actually washing John's feet! What on earth is He doing? Why would He pull a stunt like that?

That's just like Him, though. That's why He's got to go. We can't have a man claiming to be the Messiah who goes around acting like a servant. We need power. Sheer, unadulterated power. Power that will force these blasted Romans out of our land.

Won't anybody object? What kind of an image does it create for our leader to be doing the work of a servant? Hey! At last we're going to find out something. Good old Peter. You can always count on him. He's somewhat dense. Jesus calls him "Rock." That's a fair description of what's in his head. Peter's not going to let Jesus wash his feet. Even as dense as Peter is, he realizes that this isn't the kind of image we need. I'll have to talk with Peter after tonight. He may be some use to me after all.

Can you believe that! Peter's going to let Him wash his feet after all. Jesus has a strange way with words. Would you listen to that big ox! Now Peter wants Jesus to wash not only his feet but his whole body! I'd like to pour that whole pitcher of water over his head! Well, so much for using him in my new plans.

He's getting closer. How can I get out of this? I know. I'll just excuse myself and say I have to go give some money to the poor. That way I won't have to look Him in the eyes and have Him wash my feet. I don't think I can take it.

Only Andrew and Matthew to go, and He'll be at my feet. I must leave now, or it will be obvious. But if I do go, they may get suspicious. Maybe He just suspects something and is trying to force my hand and make me act. Maybe it would be better to just play it cool and let Him go ahead and wash my feet.

Hmm. The water is surprisingly warm. He is such a gentle person. If it were any other time I'm sure He and I could have been good friends. But. . . .

His hands are so gentle. Look at His back. I had never realized He had so many muscles. I guess those years of carpentry left Him strong. But He is so gentle. Look at the way He wipes my feet. Almost like a mother stroking her child. He still hasn't looked at me. Does He know? I can't stand it any longer. I think I'm going to scream. I wish He'd slap me, spit on me. Why does He keep wiping my feet? Can He hear my heart pounding?

What was that? It felt like a drop of water hit my foot. Where'd it come from? Now He's wiping it off. No! No! Please don't. He's raising His head. I can't look at Him in the face? Oh, dear God, no! Those eyes! He's been crying. He knows. But how? Who? I must get out of here before He tells the rest of the group. They'd tear me limb from limb if they knew.

He went on. He's not going to tell. Can you believe that? He's so weak that He can't even call my hand. His hands, though, . . . they were so gentle. So . . . forgiving.

Oh no, I was wrong. He's going to squeal on me after all. He said one of us is going to betray Him. He does know. But how? If I can reach my knife under my robe, at least I'll have a fighting chance to get out of here alive.

Listen to those dullards. Each one of them asking if he's the one. Well, at least, no one suspects me.

He's turning my way. I better get ready to make my break. The element of surprise. Spring to action. Move swiftly. Maybe I can make it after all. What? What's He saying? Hurry up and do what you have to do? He's not going to tell after all.

I've got to get out of here. I can't take it any more. I feel like I'm about to pass out. I must get out into the night air.

Oh, the breeze feels so good. I thought my lungs were going to burst up there. I've got to get to the Temple and meet the guards. . . . His eyes—why didn't He tell? Why did He have to look at me? Oh, well, He's got to go. It's like He said, "Whatever you do, do it quickly." If that's the way He wants it, I'll do it. But it's so dark out here. It's . . . so . . . very . . . dark!

I Believe in Jesus Christ!

Scripture Reference: Acts 2:38
Voices: 1
Time: 3:00

It is hard to believe what has happened to me today. When I woke up this morning, I never dreamed that so much could happen. I just thought it would be another Feast of Pentecost—no different than any of the others I have celebrated. Was I ever wrong! This has turned out to be the most unusual day of my life. And the most wonderful! I'm still not sure I understand what has happened. All I know is that I have met Jesus Christ, and He is now a part of my life.

I don't understand what made that loud noise this morning that sounded like a whirlwind. Nor do I understand what that strange light was that played all over the believers' heads. But it certainly got my attention. I have heard our rabbis tell of God's demand that His people confess their sin, but I had just never thought I was much of a sinner. At least, until today.

I can never forget what Peter said about our being guilty for allowing the Romans to put God's Son to death on the cross. But what really troubled me was when he said that God had made Jesus Lord and Messiah. When he said that, so many things fit together for me. All my life I had looked for the Messiah. Suddenly, I realized that He had come, and His name is Jesus! When I realized that, all my guilt seemed to come to the surface. When I asked Peter what I could do, he said that I had to turn from my sins and then be baptized in the name of Jesus. Then I would know forgiveness and peace. And he was right. The moment I said that I would do that, a feeling swept over me like a wave of water. Suddenly, I felt clean and free. All of the sacrifices I have offered over the years never made me feel like this. All of the observance of the law never gave me the feeling of peace that I have now.

There are so many people here. Someone said there were thousands of people who responded to what Peter said. I can believe that. There must be more than a hundred waiting to be baptized now.

I wonder what all those people over there think? Some of them look so upset and angry. I wish they had the peace in their lives that I have in mine. My prayer is that as they see me baptized they will somehow know that something marvelous has happened to me on the inside.

O o o o. The water is cold. Oh, thank You, God, for leading me to Jerusalem today. Thank You for forgiving me of all my sin.

What? Oh, I'm sorry. I was thinking of something else. . . . Yes! I believe Jesus Christ is God's Son, and He has forgiven me of my sin! Hallelujah!

6

Hymns Don't Have to Be Sung

One resource for creative ways to present the gospel that is often overlooked is the hymnal. The hymnal can be used for more than singing the first and last stanzas in a departmental meeting or in a worship service. It is a great source of ideas for persons seeking to add variety to lessons or programs.

Sing Them

Of course, the most familiar way to use hymns is to sing them. This is nothing new. People have been singing hymns and psalms for centuries. May it long continue!

However, give some thought in advance to what you are singing. Many hymnals have a scriptural index such as the ones found in *Baptist Hymnal* (1975) on page 544 or *The Methodist Hymnal* (1966) on page 846. If you are planning a program, use these indexes to help you correlate the hymns with the Scripture you are using. Of course every hymn does not have a specific scriptural basis, but those that do can be used.

Don't hesitate to use a hymn in the midst of a Sunday School class. You can play it from a tape or record, you can sing it as a group, or you can enlist a person to sing it.

Read Them

However, singing hymns is not the only way they can be used. Hymns can be read quite effectively. We have a layman in our church who often leads the singing on Wednesday evenings. He does a most effective thing. Instead of singing a hymn or a particular stanza, he will read it while we listen. We get accustomed to singing hymns, and sometime just to hear them read makes us think about the words.

Let me suggest that you experiment with some different ways of using hymns. Hymns can easily be made into choral readings. Those that have a line that keeps recurring are ideal choices for choral readings. Such hymns as "Let Jesus Come into Your Heart" can be adapted, letting one person or group read the stanza and the other person or group respond with the recurring line. Using hymns is a good learning activity for a large group because most churches have hymnals available for large groups.

Hymns also allow you to combine a hymn with a reading of the Bible. This reading can be interspersed between the verses ("The Lord Is My Shepherd") or read at the beginning ("Nothing but the Blood") or made into a biblical reading ("Christ the Lord Is Risen Today").

Experiment with some of the hymns in the hymnal that are not normally sung. Some of these have great messages but may be difficult to sing or unfamiliar to the group. You can use these as readings and still communicate the message.

The Lord Is My Shepherd

Scripture Reference: Psalm 23
Hymn: "The King of Love My Shepherd Is," Henry W. Baker
Voices: leader and congregation
Time: 1:30

LEADER: "The Lord is my shepherd; I shall not want."
CONGREGATION: "The King of love my Shepherd is,
              Whose goodness faileth never:
              I nothing lack if I am his
              And he is mine forever."
LEADER: "He maketh me to lie down in green pastures; he leadeth me beside the still waters. He restoreth my soul: he leadeth me in the paths of righteousness for his name's sake."
CONGREGATION: "Where streams of living water flow,
              My ransomed soul he leadeth,
              And, where the verdant pastures grow,
              With food celestial feedeth."

LEADER: "Yea, though I walk through the valley of the shadow of death, I will fear no evil: for thou art with me: thy rod and thy staff they comfort me. Thou preparest a table before me in the presence of mine enemies: thou anointest my head with oil; my cup runneth over."

CONGREGATION: "Perverse and foolish, oft I strayed,
But yet in love he sought me,
And on his shoulder gently laid,
And home, rejoicing, brought me."

LEADER: "Surely goodness and mercy shall follow me all the days of my life: and I will dwell in the house of the Lord for ever."

CONGREGATION: "And so through all the length of days
Thy goodness faileth never:
Good Shepherd, may I sing thy praise
Within thy house forever."

Christ the Lord Is Risen

Scripture Reference: Luke 24:1-6*a*
Hymn: "Christ the Lord Is Risen Today," Charles Wesley
Voices: 3 + leader and congregation
Time: 2:00

ALL: "Now upon the first day of the week,
1: "Very early in the morning,
2: "They came unto the sepulchre
3: "Bringing the spices which they had prepared,
1: "And certain others with them.
2: "And they found the stone rolled away from the sepulchre.
3: "And it came to pass,
1: "As they were much perplexed thereabout,
2 & 3: "Behold,
3: "Two men stood by them in shining garments:
1: "And as they were afraid
2:                              [afraid]
3:                                   [afraid]
1: "And bowed down their faces to the earth,
2: "They said unto them,

1 & 3: "Why seek ye the living among the dead?
1: "He is not here,
ALL: "But is risen."

LEADER: "Christ the Lord is ris'n today,
CONGREGATION: "Alleluia!
LEADER: "Sons of men and angels say,
CONGREGATION: "Alleluia!
LEADER: "Raise your joys and triumphs high,
CONGREGATION: "Alleluia!
LEADER: "Sing, ye heav'ns, and earth reply,
CONGREGATION: "Alleluia!"

LEADER: "Lives again our glorious King,
CONGREGATION: "Alleluia!
LEADER: "Where, O Death, is now thy sting?
CONGREGATION: "Alleluia!
LEADER: "Dying once he all doth save,
CONGREGATION: "Alleluia!
LEADER: "Where thy victory, O Grave?
CONGREGATION: "Alleluia!"

LEADER: "Love's redeeming work is done,
CONGREGATION: "Alleluia!
LEADER: "Fought the fight, the battle won,
CONGREGATION: "Alleluia!
LEADER: "Death in vain forbids him rise,
CONGREGATION: "Alleluia!
LEADER: "Christ hath opened Paradise,
CONGREGATION: "Alleluia!"

LEADER: "Soar we now where Christ has led,
CONGREGATION: "Alleluia!
LEADER: "Foll'wing our exalted Head,
CONGREGATION: "Alleluia!
LEADER: "Made like him, like him we rise,
CONGREGATION: "Alleluia!
LEADER: "Ours the cross, the grave, the skies,

CONGREGATION: "Alleluia!"

Nothing but the Blood

Scripture Reference: Hebrews 9:22
Hymn: "Nothing But the Blood," Robert Lowry
Voices: leader and congregation
Time: 1:00

ALL: "And almost all things are by the law purged with blood; and
    without shedding of blood is no remission" (Heb. 9:22).
1: "What can wash away my sin?
2: "Nothing but the blood of Jesus.
1: "What can make me whole again?
2: "Nothing but the blood of Jesus."

1: "For my pardon this I see,
2: "Nothing but the blood of Jesus.
1: "For my cleansing, this my plea,
2: "Nothing but the blood of Jesus."

1: "Nothing can for sin atone,
2: "Nothing but the blood of Jesus.
1: "Naught of good that I have done,
2: "Nothing but the blood of Jesus."

1: "This is all my hope and peace,
2: "Nothing but the blood of Jesus.
1: "This is all my righteousness,
2: "Nothing but the blood of Jesus."

ALL: "Oh! precious is the flow
1: "That makes me white as snow;
2: "No other fount I know,
ALL: "Nothing but the blood of Jesus."

Sweet Hour of Prayer

Scripture Reference: James 5:16
Hymn: "Sweet Hour of Prayer," William Walford
Voices: 3
Time: 1:30

1: "Sweet hour of prayer,
2: "Sweet hour of prayer,
3: "That calls me from a world of care
1: "And bids me at my Father's throne
2: "Make all my wants
3: "And wishes
2: "Known!
3: "In seasons of distress and grief,
1: "My soul has often found relief,
2: "And oft escaped the tempter's snare
3: "By thy return,
ALL: "Sweet hour of prayer."

1: "Sweet hour of prayer,
2: "Sweet hour of prayer,
3: "Thy wings shall my petition bear To him whose truth
1: "And faithfulness
2: "Engage the waiting soul to bless:
3: "And since he bids me seek his face,
1: "Believe his word
3: "And trust his grace,
2: "I'll cast on him my ev'ry care,
3: "And wait for thee,
ALL: "Sweet hour of prayer."

1: "Sweet hour of prayer,
2: "Sweet hour of prayer,
3: "May I thy consolation share,
1: "Till, from Mount Pisgah's lofty height,
2: "I view my home
1: "And take my flight:

3: "This robe of flesh I'll drop

1: "And rise To seize the everlasting prize;

2: "And shout,

1: While passing through the air,

3: " 'Farewell,

2: "Farewell,

ALL: "Sweet hour of prayer!' "

7

Biblical Simulations or Interviews

Biblical simulations are a great way to involve people in Bible study and to encourage them to think like the biblical characters. A biblical simulation seeks to thrust modern people and forms back into biblical times. Today we are quite accustomed to seeing interviews with famous people and with people who are not so famous who have witnessed some particular event. Biblical simulations allow the user to cover a lot of information and to couch it in a form that is familiar to people today. Biblical facts can be worked into the interview in such a way that the people learn without even knowing they are learning.

If you use a simulation, be sure you enlist persons to present it far enough in advance so that they will have time to thoroughly learn the material. The person who is doing the reporting will be able to use a notebook with questions written on it. However, the person(s) being interviewed will need to be so familiar with the material that he can answer the questions without notes. This means that he must have preparation time.

If you are going to write your own simulation, consider the following ideas.

- You will need a script or at least a list of questions the interviewer will ask. This means those involved will have to work together to plan the questions.
- Ask those participating to study the Scripture thoroughly. The more thoroughly they know the Scripture, the more realistic the simulation will be.
- Caution the person doing the interviewing not to throw in questions that will make the person being interviewed come out of character.
- Be careful not to include information that is contrary to the

biblical situation. The audience has no way of knowing if an answer is biblical or extrabiblical.

- Some extrabiblical facts can be used. For example, you can create a person who does not appear in the Bible to share information with the group. For example in the biblical simulation on Daniel the first character interviewed is a trusted official in King Darius's court. The character is not mentioned in the Bible, but it is certain that there were officials in the king's court that could have been interviewed. Although extrabiblical, this character is not unbelievable nor does his presence introduce information that is not true.
- Plan some time to rehearse before the presentation. This time is helpful to keep the person being interviewed from being thrown by a question.
- Use biblical simulations/interviews as a way of covering large amounts of material and introducing characters or events. Afterward, the group can divide into smaller groups and discuss the material presented.
- Although the simulation would be more effective if it is presented live, you can tape it and play it. This would enable you to use the simulation more than once.
- As a prop, you might want to have a microphone for the reporter to use.

Esther Saves Her People

Scripture Reference: Esther 3:1 to 7:10
Voices: 5
Time: 10:00

ANNOUNCER: This is station KSUS in Susa, Persia, the station that brings you all of the news while it is still news. And tonight the news is that a top government official was hanged today on gallows he had built to execute someone else. For the details of this story we go now to our eyewitness reporter on the scene at the king's palace.

REPORTER: Good evening. A sobering demonstration of how greed and hatred can backfire took place here today. Haman, the prime minister of the Persian Empire, was hanged today at his own home. The hanging was ordered by King Xerxes himself. To get the details of this most unusual story I have asked three people to join me here in our capital newsroom. First, let me introduce you to Harbona, one of the king's servants. Harbona, welcome to KSUS.

HARBONA: Thank you.

REPORTER: Harbona, would you tell us a little bit about Haman?

HARBONA: Haman had been involved in government service for several years. He had always proven to be a loyal servant. In fact, King Xerxes had just appointed him prime minister not too long ago. The king had even ordered the people to bow down to him when he passed in the street.

REPORTER: That sounds quite impressive. Can you explain the sudden change of circumstances?

HARBONA: Well, as odd as it may sound, it was this bowing that got Haman into trouble. Haman was an Agagite or Amalakite. I understand that his family had been captured several years ago and brought to Susa and he had risen rapidly in government service. However, when Haman was elevated to prime minister, there was one man who would not bow down when he passed.

REPORTER: Who was that?

HARBONA: It was Mordecai, the Jew who had saved the life of the king several years ago. Mordecai also turned out to be the cousin and foster father of Queen Esther, although none of us knew that until today.

REPORTER: Why wouldn't Mordecai bow down like everyone else?

HARBONA: There is a long-standing feud between the Jews and the Amalakites. They have been enemies for years. Although all the other Jews would bow down, Mordecai refused to do so.

REPORTER: How did Haman respond to this insult?

HARBONA: Haman became so incensed that Mordecai would not bow down when he passed by, that he went to the king and asked permission to execute not only Mordecai, but every Jew in the Persian Empire.

REPORTER: That seems like a rather severe punishment just because one Jew would not bow down.

HARBONA: Yes, it does. However, Haman apparently saw this as his chance to get rid of the Jews once and for all.

REPORTER: What kept him from carrying out his plot?

HARBONA: Mordecai got into the act. This was how we learned the relationship between Mordecai and Esther. Mordecai urged Esther to approach the king and beg for her life and the life of her people.

REPORTER: Did Haman know that Esther was Jewish?

HARBONA: Most definitely not! He had no idea of her nationality.

REPORTER: You said that Mordecai urged Esther to approach the king. All of the empire knows that is an offense punishable by death. Only those who are invited into the king's presence can see him.

HARBONA: Yes, that's true. However, there is one way out. If the king holds out his golden scepter to the person, that person is not executed.

REPORTER: That is really a risky action.

HARBONA: Yes, it was, but Esther really had no choice. She could either die when all the other Jews were killed or she could chance having the king hold out the scepter to her and save her people.

REPORTER: What did Queen Esther do?

HARBONA: I happened to be serving the king that day. Let's see, . . . it was the day before yesterday. All of a sudden I looked up and there stood Esther! She was standing just outside the throne room in the courtyard. Right where the king could see her. I held my breath waiting to see what the king would do. He suddenly smiled and extended his scepter to her. She came into the throne room and touched the end of the scepter. The king asked her what she wanted. He even offered her half of his kingdom. I could hardly believe my ears when I heard her ask the king and Haman to come to dinner that evening! I said to myself right then that something was up.

REPORTER: Thank you, Harbona. We'll return to you a little later. Right now let me move over here to our second guest. This is Deborah, one of the queen's servants. Welcome, Deborah to KSUS.

DEBORAH: Thank you.

REPORTER: Deborah, Harbona has told us what happened up to this point. I wonder if you would pick up the story from here. Were you aware that the queen was going to go see the king?

DEBORAH: Oh yes. We had known for three days. When Mordecai had urged the queen to approach the king, the queen had agreed to do it only if all the Jews would fast and pray. Naturally, the queen and all of her servants did the same.

REPORTER: Was the queen nervous about going? She really didn't be-

lieve the king would have her put to death, did she? After all she
is the queen!

DEBORAH: The queen was very nervous about going. Don't forget, the
king had deposed Vashti the previous queen because she had dis-
obeyed an order. He certainly could have been displeased by the
queen's coming to see him.

REPORTER: What happened the day she went to see the king?

DEBORAH: We spent hours making her look as beautiful as she could be.
We picked her most beautiful royal robes and did everything we
could to make her so lovely the king could not refuse her. But, most
of all, we prayed. When she walked out the door, we sat in silence,
wondering what was going to happen.

REPORTER: So you did not know what happened in the throne room
until the queen came back?

DEBORAH: That's right. When she came in she was smiling, and we all
knew she had gotten her request.

REPORTER: Why did the queen invite Haman and the king to dinner?

DEBORAH: Well, she not only invited them to dinner once, but twice. She
wanted to build the king's interest. She also was hoping that in some
way Haman would show his true colors to the king in the process.

REPORTER: Well, did he?

DEBORAH: I should say he did! He was so puffed up when he came to
dinner that first day. He looked just like a big toad sitting there
fawning before the king and queen. Then when she invited them
back the next day, I thought he was going to burst! But he sure got
his wind taken out.

REPORTER: How did that happen?

DEBORAH: When Haman left that day he passed Mordecai at the palace
gate. And, as usual, Mordecai refused to bow down like everyone
else around him. We were watching Haman as he left, and you could
see the anger on his face.

REPORTER: Thank you, Deborah. We'll get back to you in a moment.
Right now I want to welcome a friend of Haman's who was with
Haman last night. He has asked that we not identify him for fear
of repercussions. Thank you, sir, for being with us. Can you tell us
what happened when Haman came home from the palace yesterday?

MAN: He called all of his family and friends together and told us about

the delightful banquet the queen had given for the king and him.
And he was so proud that he had been invited back the next day.
When he was telling us all of this, I said to myself that something
was fishy. I know he was high up in government circles and a good
friend of the king, but he wasn't so important that the queen would
invite him twice for dinner. Something had to be up.

REPORTER: Can you tell us about the gallows Haman had built in his
yard?

MAN: After Haman had told us all about the dinner and reminded us
how important he was, he told us about leaving the palace and
meeting Mordecai. I've never seen anyone hate someone as much
as Haman hated Mordecai. We suggested that Haman build a gallows seventy-five feet tall and hang Mordecai on it before he went
back to the banquet.

REPORTER: It's obvious that he did not succeed in doing that. Can you
explain what happened?

MAN: Haman ordered some of the palace carpenters to build the gallows
that night. Then early the next morning he went to the palace to ask
the king for permission to hang Mordecai, but he never got the
chance.

REPORTER: Why?

MAN: The king had been unable to sleep last night. He had called for
the official records to be read to him, and he had discovered that
nothing had ever been done to reward Mordecai for saving his life
sometime back. When Haman entered, the king asked Haman what
he could do to honor someone and Haman, thinking the king wanted to honor him, told him.

REPORTER: Told him what?

MAN: He told him to have him dressed in royal robes, placed on the
king's own horse, and have a nobleman lead him through the city
streets crying: "See how the king rewards a man he wishes to
honor!" (Esther 6:9, GNB) Then the king told Haman to do this to
Mordecai. When Haman came back and told us what had happened, we tried to warn him then that he was in trouble, but he just
wouldn't listen to us. He got carried away with his own sense of
importance.

REPORTER: Thank you, sir. We appreciate your sharing with us this
information. Now, I want to return to Deborah, and let her finish

the story for us. Deborah, what happened when Haman came for dinner today?

DEBORAH: After the meal, while they were having their wine, the king's curiosity got the better of him. He knew all along that Esther wanted something, so he asked her what she wanted. When the queen told him that Haman had plotted to kill her and all her people, the king was furious. He was so angry that he left the room and went outside.

REPORTER: What was Haman's reaction to all of this?

DEBORAH: When Haman realized his predicament, the queen was still reclining on her couch where they had been eating. Haman threw himself on her couch to beg for his life just as the king walked back in. When the king saw Haman, he cried out, "Is this man going to rape the queen right here in front of me, in my own palace?" (Esther 7:8, GNB). When he said that he called the guards.

REPORTER: Thank you, Deborah. Now let's get back to Harbona. Harbona I understand you were in on the arrest. Would you tell us what happened at this point?

HARBONA: We were standing just outside the door when the king rushed out. When he returned, we followed him. When he saw Haman on the queen's couch, we grabbed him and covered his head, in preparation for the execution. I had heard that Haman had built the gallows, and I mentioned that to the king. He ordered us to hang Haman on the gallows that he had built for Mordecai. So we took him immediately and executed him. As far as I'm concerned, it is good riddance.

REPORTER: Harbona, possibly you can answer this question. What happens now? The king has issued an order that all the Jews be executed. He cannot take it back. What will happen? Surely he will not let his queen be killed, will he?

HARBONA: I don't know what will happen. All I know is that it looks bad for the Jews. But their God seems to take care of them. I suppose He will be able to get them out of this mess too, although I don't see how.

REPORTER: Thank you all for being with us. We will continue to keep you updated on events as they develop in this situation. As soon as we get information, we will be back with you live. Right now, this is your eyewitness reporter from the palace returning you to the station. Keep tuned to station KSUS for all the news.

Note

1. See the study guide on page 124 to be used with this simulation.

Daniel in the Lion's Den

Scripture Reference: Daniel 6:1-24, GNB
Voices: 5
Time: 8:30

REPORTER: This is your roving eyewitness reporter for station KBAB in Babylon in front of the king's palace. Just moments ago we learned that there is a plot to convict one of the high officials of treason. We have with us one of the officials of the King Darius's court. Thank you for taking time to share with our listeners what has happened. Can you tell us what is going on?

OFFICIAL: Yes, Daniel, one of the three presidents of the nation, has been accused of treason.

REPORTER: But isn't Daniel one of King Darius's most trusted advisers?

OFFICIAL: Yes, he is. That's part of the problem. Daniel is a foreigner, and some of the other court officials do not like that.

REPORTER: Would you say that they are jealous of Daniel?

OFFICIAL: Well, . . . yes. That's why they hatched this plot.

REPORTER: What plot? Can you describe what they are doing?

OFFICIAL: They are trying to catch Daniel in some act that would prove him to be disloyal to the king.

REPORTER: Did they find anything?

OFFICIAL: No, but they designed a scheme that would make Daniel look treasonous.

REPORTER: How did they do that if Daniel is so loyal to the king?

OFFICIAL: They petitioned the king to forbid worship or prayer to any god but the king for a period of thirty days.

REPORTER: That doesn't seem like too serious a plot.

OFFICIAL: I mentioned that Daniel is a foreigner. He is a Jew, and the Jews refuse to pray to anyone or anything but their God, Yahweh.

Daniel is completely faithful to the king, but he is also a very religious man.

REPORTER: What is the penalty for praying to some other god than the king?

OFFICIAL: Anyone found guilty of praying to any other god than the king is to be thrown into the lions' den.

REPORTER: That sounds like a rather severe penalty. Can you tell us what Daniel's reaction was to this decree?

OFFICIAL: I can only tell you what I heard. The king and his attendants rushed out of here just a short time ago. It is rumored that Daniel was seen praying in his house. Now that is just a rumor. I cannot really confirm it.

REPORTER: Thank you for your information. Let's get over to Daniel's house and see if we can find out what is happening there. I understand that there is a crowd gathering outside Daniel's house. We'll break for a commercial and then be right back, live from Daniel's house.

Here we are again, ladies and gentlemen, station KBAB in Babylon. We are continuing our coverage of the Daniel treason episode. Excuse me, ma'am. I understand that there has been a bit of commotion here. Can you tell me what happened?

WOMAN: Yes, I can. I saw the whole thing from my house across the street.

REPORTER: Would you tell our audience what you saw?

WOMAN: I was looking out of my window—that one right there that faces Daniel's house—when I saw Daniel pull the curtains back and kneel down and start praying.

REPORTER: Was he praying to anything? Was there a statue of the king or any other god?

WOMAN: No, he was facing in the direction of Jerusalem where he used to live before he was taken prisoner. That's the way with these foreigners. They come in here and just take over. They start trying to change things. If he wants to live here, he needs to worship our gods and leave his gods at home. They must not have been too powerful or he would still be living in Jerusalem.

REPORTER: Was that all that happened?

WOMAN: That was all that happened that time, but the second time he did it, there were some guards from the palace here.

REPORTER: How did they find out about Daniel?

WOMAN: They came after the hour of morning prayer. This time when he came to the window to pray, they were watching. As soon as he started praying, they rushed in and arrested him.

REPORTER: How long ago was that?

WOMAN: Just a short time ago. I understand that they have taken him to the lions' den. And I say good riddance. Maybe that'll teach those foreigners they can't come in here with all their strange ways. That ought to really put the fear of the gods in them. We'll see how strong their God really is!

REPORTER: Thank you, ma'am. There is a palace guard standing in the doorway of Daniel's house. Let's see if he can give us any additional information about Daniel. Excuse me, Sir, I wonder if we could have just a minute of your time to ask you some questions about what happened here this morning.

GUARD: Sure. I just don't want my name mentioned.

REPORTER: Fine. You are a member of the palace guard, is that correct?

GUARD: Yes, it is.

REPORTER: Were you here at the time of the arrest?

GUARD: Yes, I was.

REPORTER: Could you tell us exactly what happened?

GUARD: We received a report at the palace this morning that Daniel had been seen praying in spite of the order that no one could pray to any god except the king. As you know this is against the law of the Medes and Persians.

REPORTER: How did King Darius react to this? I understand that Daniel is one of his most trusted colleagues.

GUARD: Well, the king was rather upset, because he realized that he had been tricked. When he had signed the law, he had no intention of losing one of his best supporters.

REPORTER: Wasn't there anything the king could do?

GUARD: No, not even the king can change the law after it has been made.

REPORTER: What happened then?

GUARD: The king was forced to carry out his order. He commanded Daniel to be thrown into the lions' den.

REPORTER: Did you hear the king say anything to Daniel?

GUARD: Yes, he told Daniel that he believed that his God would be great enough to save him.

REPORTER: Thank you, Sir, for your information. You have been very helpful. We'll break now, and I'll be back to you live just as soon as I can get to the lions' den.

Ladies and gentlemen, this is your roving reporter for station KBAB in Babylon. If you have been listening to our report, you know that we have kept a vigil here all night long. We are just outside the lions' den on the edge of town. In the den are lions and Daniel, one of the top three members of the kings' advisory council. Daniel was placed there because he refused to obey an order not to pray to anyone but King Darius for a period of thirty days. Daniel was thrown in the den last night. The door has been sealed with the official seal so no one can get into it but the king. I have checked with the guards here, and there is no other entrance in or out of the den but through this one right in front of me. As I said, I have been here all night. We have heard absolutely no sounds coming from the den. No one has gone near the door. The guards have absolutely refused to let us even get close. Wait a minute. Someone is coming. I believe it's the king. Excuse me, King Darius, would you answer a few questions for our listeners? I'm sure this whole business must have greatly upset you.

KING: Yes, it has. I did not sleep or eat anything all night. I'm sorry, I don't have time for more questions. I must find out what happened to Daniel.

REPORTER: Thank you, Sir, we won't detain you. We're interested in what happened to Daniel too. Go right ahead, sir. We'll watch.

(*Aside to the audience*) The king is now going over to the large stone door covering the den. He is inspecting the seal. It is still intact. It has not been broken. He has now ordered the guards to move the stone. He's peering into the darkness of the den. We still have heard no sound. Now he's calling for Daniel: "Daniel, servant of the living God! Was the God you serve so loyally able to save you from the lions?" What's that? A voice from the den said, "O king, live for ever!" It sounded like Daniel's voice. He *is* alive! He said that he was alive and well and that his God had protected him because he had not sinned against either Him or the king. I can't believe it! No one has ever spent the night in a den of lions and lived to tell about it. They're bringing Daniel out right now. We'll try to get an interview with him just as soon as we can. Right now we must break for station identification. This is your roving, eyewitness reporter in Babylon at the lions' den.

The Arrest of Jesus

Scripture References: John 18:1-27 (Matt. 26:47 to 27:10; Mark 14:43-72; Luke 22:47-62)

Voices: 4

Time: 9:00

REPORTER: This is your roving eyewitness reporter for station WJER in Jerusalem. Many events have happened here tonight. Things have developed so quickly that we have not had time to get all of the details. However, I'm going to see if we can interview some of the people who have been involved in tonight's events. First, let me give you a little background information. Over the past several months, the name of Jesus of Nazareth has become a household word here in Jerusalem. He has collected quite a following not only in Nazareth and Galilee but here in Jerusalem as well. Most of His followers have been among the common people. He has attracted few community leaders, although there are rumors that some of the Sanhedrin are numbered among His followers.

This support from the common people has upset the Sanhedrin. They have sought on numerous occasions to trap Jesus into making some kind of statement that would enable them to arrest Him.

Tonight that arrest has occurred. As I said earlier, we are not quite sure of all the details, but we will try to bring these to you as the story continues to unfold. We do know that one of Jesus' own disciples betrayed Him. Right now, that is all the information we know, but some of our staff are trying to locate him and as soon as they do we will interview him.

Right now, we're here in the courtyard of Caiaphas, the high priest. It is our understanding that Jesus is inside being interrogated by the council. As information is available on Him, we'll share it with you. Many of the people here in the courtyard were involved in the events of the evening. Here is one of the Temple guards who was involved in the arrest.

Pardon me, sir. I wonder if I could ask you a few questions about the arrest you made tonight? Would you please tell our audience what happened?

GUARD: Well, we received orders just a few hours ago to be on the alert. We couldn't even go home to get ready for the Passover tomorrow. We knew something big was up.

REPORTER: Something big?

GUARD: Yes, something big. In fact, I'm not sure I really understand all that happened.

REPORTER: Well, what did happen?

GUARD: We were ordered to go to the Garden of Gethsemane and . . .

REPORTER: Excuse me, but who issued the order?

GUARD: I'm not really sure who actually issued the order. All I know is that it came from the high priest's house.

REPORTER: What did the order tell you to do?

GUARD: It told us to go to the Garden of Gethsemane and arrest Jesus of Nazareth.

REPORTER: Was that all?

GUARD: Yes, that was all. Oh, we were told that one of Jesus' followers would lead us so we could identify Jesus in the darkness. Even with the full moon it is still dark among all those olive trees.

REPORTER: Who was this disciple?

GUARD: His name is Judas. He is from the small town of Kerioth, about thirty to thirty-five miles south of Jerusalem.

REPORTER: What else do you know about Judas?

GUARD: Nothing else.

REPORTER: Do you have any idea why he would turn on his friend and teacher?

GUARD: No, I thought it kind of strange myself. There was a rumor among the guards that he had gotten some money for it. It must have been a great amount to sell out his teacher.

REPORTER: What happened when you got to the Garden of Gethsemane?

GUARD: Well, apparently Jesus had seen us coming. He was standing in a little clearing waiting for us.

REPORTER: You mean to say He didn't try to run away or hide? That doesn't sound like a fugitive to me.

GUARD: That was what bothered me. He really didn't act like a fugitive, either. Judas walked up to Jesus, greeted Him, and then kissed Him. And then we arrested Him.

REPORTER: Was that all? I heard reports of some other strange happenings.

GUARD: Well, . . . It all happened so quickly, and it was dark, that I didn't see it happen.

REPORTER: See what happen?

GUARD: The miracle.

REPORTER: What do you mean "miracle"? Would you please explain to our listeners?

GUARD: Well, one of the followers of this Jesus, named Simon Peter, had a sword, and he pulled it out and swung at Malchus the servant of the high priest, Caiaphas.

REPORTER: Did he hurt him?

GUARD: Well, yes and no.

REPORTER: Come now, my friend. He either hurt him or he didn't hurt him.

GUARD: Well, he cut off his ear. Peter swung at his head, and Malchus ducked, and Peter sliced his ear off as slick as could be. I shudder to think what would have happened if Malchus had not ducked.

REPORTER: What happened then?

GUARD: We started to attack Peter, but Jesus stopped us, stooped down and picked up Malchus's ear, and placed it back on his head.

REPORTER: Thank you for sharing with us your account of these events. I have just received word that Malchus is still here in the courtyard. Let me make my way over to him. While I'm doing that let me remind you that we are still trying to locate this Judas Iscariot. By the way, I caught a glimpse of Jesus as He was being led into the Sanhedrin. We'll see if we can give you a report on Him and what the Sanhedrin has decided. But, first, here is Malchus. Good evening, Malchus, and welcome to WJER. I understand that you have had quite an experience tonight. Would you tell our listeners what happened?

MALCHUS: I am still a little shaky, but I will try to tell you what happened. I was with the group that had gone to arrest Jesus. In fact, Caiaphas had sent me to be certain that the arrest went as it was planned. We got to the Garden and Judas walked up to Jesus, and kissed Him. That was our agreed-upon signal so we would not get the wrong man in the darkness. I happened to be standing next to Judas, when, all of a sudden, I caught a glimpse of something flashing in the moonlight. Instinctively, I ducked, and then I felt a searing pain in my right ear. I screamed, and the guards lunged for a man who was holding a sword. I grabbed my head and realized my ear was gone! The pain was intense.

REPORTER: You mean that you actually had your ear severed by a sword? It looks perfectly whole now.

MALCHUS: That's the part I still do not understand. The guards grabbed the man with the sword, then Jesus just held up His hand and told Peter to put up his sword. Jesus called for a torch so He could see, and He reached down and picked up my ear from off the ground and placed it back on my head. Immediately the pain disappeared.

REPORTER: Why would Jesus do that? I thought you were there to arrest Him?

MALCHUS: We were. I really don't understand it either. All I know is that I lost my ear, and Jesus put it back on my head.

REPORTER: What did you do to Peter?

MALCHUS: Well, nothing. Jesus asked us to let him and all the others go, and we really did not have any reason to arrest them, so we let them all go. You'll have to excuse me. I am still shaken up by everything that has happened tonight. I must get some rest.

REPORTER: Thanks, Malchus, we wish you a speedy recovery. We still have not been able to locate Judas Iscariot. We have learned that he was the treasurer of the group. As soon as we find him we will try to get an interview with him. The latest report is that someone resembling him was seen near the edge of town. We are checking out the report.

I understand that a man who resembles Simon Peter who wielded the sword has been spotted here in the courtyard. Let's see if we can get over to him and get his side of the story. This courtyard is a busy place tonight. Pardon me. Let me through. Ah, there he is by the fire, warming his hands. Excuse me, sir. I understand that you may be one of the followers of Jesus of Nazareth. Is that correct?

PETER: Jesus of Nazareth? I've never even heard of the man!

REPORTER: But, sir, we have been told by very credible sources that you were with him tonight in the Garden of Gethsemane.

PETER: I have no comment.

REPORTER: But surely you don't deny that you are one of His followers.

PETER: I swear to you by the God of heaven that I have never even heard of the man!

REPORTER: All right, thank you, Sir. Well, the drama continues to unfold. A man cuts off the ear of the servant of the high priest in defending his teacher, and then he denies that he even knows the man. Excuse me a moment. Mmmm. The events of the night take on a more serious cast. As you know, we have been trying to locate Judas Iscariot all night so we can discover why he would turn against a friend and teacher. I'm afraid we will never know the answer to that question. His body was found just moments ago hanging from the limb of a tree near the edge of the city. We will break now, and we'll be back live just as soon as I can get over to the scene of Judas' apparent suicide. This is your eyewitness reporter for station WJER, Jerusalem.

It Happened at Pentecost

Scripture Reference: Acts 2:1-42
Voices: 4
Time: 8:00

REPORTER: This is your eyewitness reporter for station WJER in Jerusalem. Jerusalem is no stranger to unusual happenings. In recent weeks we have reported to you several events, all of them having to do with a man named Jesus of Nazareth. You may recall that He was crucified by the Roman government, but His disciples claim that He came back to life. His followers, instead of disappearing, have continued to grow in number. Today's events appear to be the latest development in this spectacular situation. It has been exactly seven weeks since the followers of Jesus claimed He rose from the dead. Today, on this Feast of Pentecost, strange things have happened here in Jerusalem. And, as it is our policy to bring you all the news, we want to interview some of the people involved in this event.

I have with me Publius Titus. Publius, thank you for being with us today. Would you tell our listeners what you do?

PUBLIUS: I am a Roman soldier assigned to Caesarea, but temporarily on duty here in Jerusalem.

REPORTER: How long have you been here in Jerusalem?

PUBLIUS: About three months, now. We were sent over just before the Passover to help keep order just in case any problems broke out.

REPORTER: Why are you still here?

PUBLIUS: Well, ever since the Passover and the execution of Jesus of Nazareth, strange things have been happening.

REPORTER: I understand some strange things happened here today. Would you describe them for us?

PUBLIUS: That is difficult to do, because I'm not a religious person by nature.

REPORTER: Well, from your perspective, would you tell us what you saw?

PUBLIUS: I was assigned to patrol the streets. As I came near the house of John Mark, I saw . . .

REPORTER: Excuse me for interrupting, but why were you patrolling in front of the house of John Mark?

PUBLIUS: That is one of the chief gathering places for the followers of this Jesus fellow. Ever since they met there the night before He was executed, His followers have continued to use the house as a gathering place. We have kept it under surveillance ever since. As I was saying, when I came near the house of John Mark, I saw people running toward the house from all directions. I ran to get near the house, thinking that some kind of violence was about to break out. But when I got there, all I heard was one of the leaders of the group who was talking.

REPORTER: Was there anything strange about that?

PUBLIUS: Not really. At least I didn't think so at first. He was speaking in Latin. At first that didn't even strike me as unusual. That is the language I had grown up speaking. Then I realized that the speaker was a Galilean fisherman who had never been outside the country. Where could he have learned Latin?

REPORTER: Latin? What good would that have done for him to speak in Latin? Few people in this crowd could understand it.

PUBLIUS: Well, that's where the strangeness comes in. There were others standing there who claimed they heard him speaking in Egyptian. Others said he was speaking Arabic. Still others said they heard him speaking in their language. But I know he was speaking in Latin. I heard him. I have not heard a Jew in Jerusalem speak Latin since I have been here. And he did not have an accent, either!

REPORTER: What you have told us is difficult to believe. Do you have any explanation for this strange event?

PUBLIUS: No, I really cannot explain it. Later, the leader of the group, Simon Peter, said it had something to do with Jesus of Nazareth. I don't understand all of the religious side of this. I only know I heard this man speaking in Latin.

REPORTER: Thank you, Publius, for your report. In just a moment, we are going to try to get inside John Mark's house and interview Simon Peter to get his side of the story. Right now let's see if we can talk with some of these people here in the street.

Pardon me, Ma'am. Were you here earlier this morning when Simon Peter preached?

WOMAN: Is that what you call it?

REPORTER: I take it that you were not too impressed with the events?

WOMAN: Impressed! I should say not! Why should I be impressed by seeing a bunch of drunks weaving and hollering and waving their arms? I see that all the time down in the marketplace.

REPORTER: You think they were all drunk?

WOMAN: Yes. This bunch does some strange things. I understand they drink blood to represent their dead leader. You know how repugnant that is for Jews. They probably were out of their heads. That illiterate fisherman who was speaking tried to say it was only nine o'clock in the morning so they couldn't be drunk. I guess he's never seen anyone on a real drunk like I have. My first husband used to.
. . .

REPORTER: Thank you, Ma'am. I appreciate your sharing your opinions with our audience. How about you, sir? Were you here this morning when all of this excitement took place?

MAN: Yes, I was. I had just gotten into the city from Crete. I have wanted to come to Jerusalem for Pentecost for several years. I had just arrived when I saw all these people running toward the house. I got caught up in the crowd. When we got up close, I saw a man standing at the balcony window and heard him talking in my own native language. Of course I was interested in hearing what someone who spoke my native dialect had to say.

REPORTER: Well, what did he say?

MAN: About that time Simon Peter—he's sort of the leader of the group—started talking. He told about all the wonderful things that God had done through the ages. He told of God's attempt to reach out to our nation, the Jews. Then he said that Jesus of Nazareth was God's Messiah or Anointed One. I had heard of Jesus, but I did not know that God had sent Him. Then Peter pointed out that God had made Jesus Lord, and that we had to repent of our sins and believe that Jesus is God's Son.

REPORTER: What was the reaction of the people?

MAN: Well, . . . Peter's words had a strange effect on the whole crowd. People all over the crowd were crying out and asking what they could do.

REPORTER: What did Peter do?

MAN: Not only Peter but all the other believers started talking to those who were interested, telling us more about Jesus.

REPORTER: What did they tell you?

MAN: They told us the best news I have ever heard. They said that Jesus had died for our sins. He was the sacrifice for all our wrongs. If we would believe that, then God would forgive our sins and Jesus would come to live in our lives through His Spirit.

REPORTER: Did you believe?

MAN: Yes! I did believe! Jesus came into my life and for the first time that I can ever remember, I have peace and joy.

REPORTER: Is that all you have to do? Just believe?

MAN: Yes, that's all. Well, there is one other thing. Because we have believed we are asked to show that by being immersed in water. That way all of the city can see that we have believed. I understand there are over three thousand people who are to be immersed this afternoon. I am on my way now to Gihon Spring for the ceremony. Why don't you come along and see the service for yourself?

REPORTER: Thank you, I believe I will. We shall return to you live just as soon as I can get to Gihon Spring where this ceremony is going to take place. In the meantime, this is your eyewitness reporter for station WJER in front of John Mark's house in Jerusalem where unusual things continue to happen involving this man Jesus. A question that has haunted all of us is this: Is Jesus really dead?

8

Pantomime as a Way to Present the Gospel

Pantomime is an ancient art. It is not often applied to religious drama today, but it can be an effective way to communicate a biblical account. Pantomime is the ability to express a story without words by using simple, symbolic gestures that are often exaggerated. Since props are not needed, this makes pantomime an excellent tool for presenting the gospel in a Sunday School class or in a worship service. Pantomime can be performed anywhere: inside or outside; in a large auditorium or small classroom; in front of a large group or in the presence of a small class; for children or for adults.

The word *pantomime* literally means "he who plays every role." A pantomimist is one who imitates all persons or all things. The original pantomimists would play different roles and indicate this by wearing a different mask for each role. For our purposes it is not necessary to wear masks. However, one can pantomime putting on a mask so the audience will be aware that a different character is being portrayed.

We get so accustomed to hearing words spoken that often they lose their effectiveness. That is what makes pantomiming so useful. The pantomimist is able to "say" something with actions that will carry a greater message than the spoken word.

Ways to Use Pantomime

Pantomime can be used in several different ways as an effective tool to present the gospel.

In the Classroom

Pantomime can be used to present certain passages of Scripture. Of course, Scriptures that include action are much easier to mime, but the

105

ancients would often mime the creation of the world. However, it would be difficult to mime the eighth chapter of Romans.

The Scripture can be read and then have the pantomimist present the mime. Or the pantomime can be presented first and then the Scripture can be read as a way of introducing the lesson. If you feel the need to introduce the pantomime, you can say something like, "I wonder what David felt when he tried on Saul's armor?"

The teacher can let class members develop their own pantomimes and let them act them out for the rest of the class. This would work especially well for children and youth, but some adult groups would also benefit from this type of activity.

In the Worship Service

Pantomime can also have a place in a worship service. The text of the sermon could be mimed, or a story or event that would relate to the sermon could be used.

As a Devotional

Often a pantomime can be used as a way of presenting a devotional thought at a retreat or fellowship. The retreat setting often provides unique opportunities for using these types of creative ideas.

Other Uses

Pantomiming can have other uses. It can be used to interpret music or Scripture as it is being read. It is a dramatic form that can span language and culture. A person who does not understand English can understand love and forgiveness when mimed effectively. Pantomiming can also span the generation gap. Children as well as adults can relate to a pantomimist.

Guidelines for Pantomiming

Pantomiming is a different form of drama, and it requires a different method of presentation. While certain basic dramatic principles would apply, pantomiming has several specific guidelines that may not apply to other dramatic forms.

1. Use simple, but exaggerated actions. Make your actions big so the

audience will be sure to see them. Eliminate all unnecessary actions. Unnecessary actions tend to confuse the audience.

2. A good way to determine if your actions are effective is to ask: If I were sitting in the audience and did not know anything about what I was doing, would I understand what is going on?

3. When you end a scene, make some definite break. Use some action to indicate that you have stopped acting and are leaving the stage. You do not want your audience to think that your walking offstage is a part of the pantomime if you are already finished. When you have finished you can freeze your actions for five to ten seconds, resume your normal appearance, and walk away. Or you can bow your head for a moment and then resume your normal appearance.

4. Early pantomimists played many different roles. Although this may be difficult for someone just beginning, it is an effective procedure. If you are going to mime more than one character ("The Good Samaritan"), you can do so by pretending to take off one mask and put on a different one for each character you portray. Even more important than the mask are the facial features and the body actions that indicate you are now a different person.

5. If you are portraying a biblical scene, you probably do not want to be humorous. Be careful not to let your exaggerated actions become ridiculous so that your audience laughs instead of understanding the point. Your purpose is not to entertain, but to teach. However, the Bible does contain some humorous passages. These make good pantomimes. An effective pantomimist can make a humorous point by miming the story Jesus told of the man who had a timber in his eye who was trying to get a speck out of the eye of another person (Matt. 7:3-5). In this case humor is intended. The gross exaggeration makes Jesus' point. That is particularly suited to pantomiming.

6. Do not think of yourself as playing charades in which you are trying to get your audience to guess what you are doing or who you are. Instead, think of yourself as a dramatist portraying a biblical scene.

7. It is not necessary to use props or sound. These can be pantomimed as well. If you choose to use props, keep them simple. You might want to use chairs ("A Warning Against Prejudice") or a table, but most of the time it is not necessary—and may even be distracting—to use props.

8. When your pantomime calls for you to speak, you can move your lips, but it is not necessary for you to mouth the exact words. You do

not need to exaggerate your lips so the audience can lip read what you are saying. Your other actions and facial features should communicate the conversation.

9. Don't look directly at the audience. Look just a little over their heads. This will keep you from being distracted by someone in the audience and also provide a little "distance" for you from the audience. This is especially helpful if you are presenting in a small Sunday School class.

10. Remember that all action must be done facing the audience. The audience must be able to see everything you do. For example, in "A Woman Receives Forgiveness," pretend that Jesus has His back to the audience so you are facing the audience directly.

11. Remember that the audience has no words to understand your message. The only way they will be able to understand what you are trying to communicate is by your actions. Be sure your actions are visible, deliberate, understandable, and significant.

12. Keep the pantomimes short—three to five minutes. This seems to be about right to make an impact on the audience. It also enables the pantomimist to memorize the actions without having to refer to any notes.

13. Your purpose is not to entertain; your purpose is to present the gospel. The message stays the same; the medium only is changed. Be certain that the message does not get lost in the medium.

14. As with any other medium used to present the gospel, you must thoroughly immerse yourself in the Scripture. Read it. Study it. Read several translations to be sure you have grasped what it is saying. When speaking, speakers use words that listeners may not grasp completely but can pick up from the context. In pantomiming if you do not understand what you are doing, no one else will either.

15. Be sure you practice before you present. The more times you have gone over what you are going to do, the more relaxed you will feel when you present it. Practice your actions and movements until you feel comfortable with doing them. If you do not feel comfortable with a particular action, change it. It will look uncomfortable to your audience if you feel uncomfortable with it.

16. Pantomiming, even more so than spoken forms of drama, forces the performer to get into the other person's skin, to try as much as possible to understand how the other person feels and what that person

is thinking. Not only will it be interesting for the audience, it will also be a real help to the person who makes the presentation. Both audience and pantomimist will remember the Scripture longer than if it is just read. After all, isn't that what real teaching is all about?

With these guidelines in mind, try your hand (and body!) at some of these suggestions. After you have gotten into practice, you can pick up nearly any event that has some action and mime it. The following suggestions will get you started. Most will take two to three minutes.

A Blind Man Sees

Scripture Reference: Luke 18:35-43 (Matt. 20:29-34; Mark 10:46-52)
Persons: 1

Scene 1

While sitting beside the road begging, you hear something in the distance. Cup your hand to your ear and listen. Turn and ask someone who it is. At first you do not understand, and then you realize who it is and you nod in vigorous agreement.

Scene 2

Jesus is nearly in front of you. Begin to call out to Jesus louder and louder. Then stop, and point to yourself as if to ask, "Who, me?" as if responding to Jesus' question as to what you want.

Scene 3

Jump up, throw off your cloak, and start groping your way toward Jesus. Respond to Jesus' questions by telling Him you want to see. Then portray the awesomeness of being able to see. Express your joy and gratitude to Jesus as you walk offstage with Him.

Warning Against Prejudice

Scripture Reference: James 2:1-9
Persons: 1

Scene 1

(*In this situation you will need chairs set up in a circle.*) A person comes in to a Sunday School classroom and is seated near the door. A second person enters who is dirty and poor. The pantomimist can indicate this by asides to the audience and by gestures referring to clothes and status. The pantomimist barely acknowledges this poor man's presence and gradually moves away from the poor person.

Scene 2

A well-dressed person enters. Again, the pantomimist describes the dress of the rich person by using exaggerated hand and facial manner-isms. This time the pantomimist is quite attentive, even fawning. The pantomimist offers the well-dressed person a seat, hands him a book, pats him on the shoulder.

Scene 3

The pantomimist listens to a teacher teach, nods occasionally, but spends more time looking at the person sitting beside him. When the class is over he ushers the rich person out of the room, pushing the poor person aside, glancing back with a look of disgust at the poor person as he goes out of the door.

A Lost Sheep Is Found

Scripture Reference: Luke 15:4-7
Persons: 1

Scene 1

With a shepherd's crook in your hand, wander around as though you are looking for a lost sheep. Portray the frustration of not being able to find it. Remember that you are looking for a live animal. Look in places where a large object would be. Let this go on for about twenty to twenty-five seconds.

Scene 2

Climb up a steep mountain. Keep looking. Then spot the sheep. Speak words of encouragement to it. Try to edge closer to the sheep as though it were on a ledge. Then, with your shepherd's crook, reach out and gently pull the sheep toward you. Hold it in your arms and reassure it.

Scene 3

Walk back into town holding the sheep and calling out to your neighbors that you have found it. Hold up the sheep for all to see and express your joy over finding it.

A Shepherd Goes to the Manger

Scripture Reference: Luke 2:8-20
Persons: 1

Scene 1

As you sit beside a campfire, an angel suddenly appears and tells you about the birth of Jesus in Bethlehem. After the angel is gone, talk with the rest of the shepherds, telling them the baby will be born in a manger.

Scene 2

Enter as though looking for a manger. Then point to the other side of the room and run to it and bow down. Peer into the manger and look at the baby. Talk with Mary and Joseph about the baby.

Scene 3

Return to the field, telling everyone that you meet along the way about the wonderful thing you have seen. Point back to the manger and tell them how they can find Jesus.

A Woman Receives Forgiveness

Scripture Reference: John 8:1-11
Persons: 1

Scene 1

A woman enters as though being dragged by someone else. She is thrown to the floor in front of Jesus. She slaps at her captor's hands as he tries to pull her up, and makes a big issue of telling him to keep his hands off of her. She is defiant and angry. She looks at her captor and mimics him as he tells Jesus of her sin. She looks back and forth between him and Jesus.

Scene 2

The woman looks at Jesus defiantly to see what He will do. She brings her gaze down to the floor level as Jesus kneels. Gradually she softens in her attitude and bows her head in her arms and sobs.

Scene 3

She looks up in response to Jesus' question. She looks all around and then shakes her head from side to side to indicate that no one has stayed around to accuse her. Then hesitantly she takes the offered hand of Jesus who helps her up to her feet. She stands for a moment not quite sure what to do. She makes a couple of false starts toward Jesus. Then she throws her arms around Jesus, and then runs offstage.

David Prepares for Battle

Scripture Reference: 1 Samuel 17:1-54
Persons: 1

Scene 1

David goes to see his brothers, and when he arrives, he sees Goliath parading around. He describes how big Goliath is. Then David indicates that he will fight him. David describes how strong he is by telling about killing a bear that came to him by grabbing it by the throat and beating it to death.

Scene 2

David tells Saul that he will fight Goliath. Saul gives David his armor to wear. David puts on all of the armor piece by piece. Last of all, he straps on Saul's sword. Then he tries to move but is just barely able to do so. He takes the armor off and explains to Saul that he will fight Goliath with his sling. He twirls his sling around his head to indicate his plan. (NOTE: *A sling is made of two leather thongs with a small leather pocket tied between the two thongs in which a rock is placed. This is swung over the head and then one thong is released and the rock flies out at a fantastic speed.*)

Scene 3

David starts toward Goliath. He stoops and picks up five small stones about the size of golf balls. He places these in a pouch at his side. As he meets Goliath, he circles cautiously and then reaches in his pouch and pulls out a stone. He places it in the sling, twirls it over his head several times, and then lets the stone fly. He runs to Goliath, places his foot on him, and looks up victoriously to God, and then bows his head.

The Good Samaritan

Scripture Reference: Luke 10:25-35
Persons: 1

Scene 1: The Priest

As you walk along the road, you see a wounded man in the ditch. React with horror. Immediately reach for your billfold or purse. Peer toward the man. Edge a little closer. Show a struggle over what to do. Look at your watch. Start to move on down the road.

Scene 2: The Levite

Walk along singing or whistling. When you see the wounded man, stop. Edge closer. Go over and touch him with your finger, and recoil in horror. Move quickly down the road.

Scene 3: The Samaritan

Saunter along the road in somewhat of a carefree manner leading a donkey. When you see the wounded man, look hurt but show compassion. Run to him. Hold up his head. Give him a drink. Tear your robe into bandages and tie up his wounds. Help him up. Steady him. Let him lean against your shoulder. Help him get on your donkey. Check to be sure he is comfortable, and then lead the donkey to the inn. Knock at the door of the inn. Explain to the innkeeper who the man is and how you found him. Tell the innkeeper to provide for him and you will pay for the care. Give the innkeeper some money. Help the wounded man from the donkey and into bed. Tell him you'll be back to see him. Pick up the reins of your donkey and lead him offstage.

Ideas to Develop

Nearly any Scripture that involves action can be pantomimed. The following should give you some ideas for developing your own.

Abraham Offering Isaac (Gen. 22:1-19)
Esau Selling His Birthright (Gen. 25:27-34)
Moses at the Burning Bush (Ex. 3:1-22)
The Twelve Spies Return (Num. 13:1-33)
The Death of Samson (Judg. 16:23-30)
Hannah Prays for a Child (1 Sam. 1:1-18)
Nehemiah Builds the Wall (Neh. 4:1-23)
Isaiah Sees the Lord (Isa. 6:1-8)
The Woman Who Touched Jesus' Cloak (Matt. 9:20-22)
The Rich Young Ruler (Mark 10:17-22; Matt. 19:16-22; Luke 18:18-23)
The Woman of Samaria (John 4:1-41)
Paul's Conversion (Acts 9:1-19; 22:6-16; 26:12-18)

In addition to these biblical passages, you can develop ideas on certain themes. Instead of writing a case study on a certain theme, develop a pantomime about that theme to introduce your lesson. The following should get you started.

A Christian tries to get enough courage to witness.
A Christian refuses a drink at a social gathering.
A parent demonstrates to a child how much he loves him.
A person tells another that he was wrong and asks to be forgiven.
A person is tempted to steal something from a department store.
A person is tempted to cheat on a test.

Pantomiming is just one more way to present the exciting gospel of Christ. Of course there can be no new gospel. It is the old gospel that we convey; we only seek to present it in a way that will catch the attention of people who have heard the gospel through the old forms so often that they are not arrested by its marvelous news. The greatest pantomime of all time was acted out on top of a hill outside the city of Jerusalem nearly two thousand years ago. There God said in unmistakable language to a lost world, "I love you!"

9

Potpourri

This chapter offers examples of several different ways to present the gospel. They range all the way from puzzles to a brief life situation. However, each form can be used to accomplish a specific purpose. Again, be sure the form you use fits the situation.

Case Studies

Case studies allow members to examine a situation that relates to their lives and to suggest ways to solve the problem. There are many different forms of case studies. The life situations in this chapter are a type of unfinished case study. Case studies are excellent ways to open or close a lesson. They grab persons and pull them into the discussion quickly. Few people wake up on Sunday morning wondering what happened to a biblical character. However, most people wake up wondering what to do with their lives. Case studies help bridge the gap between life and the Bible. This bridge then allows the teacher to bring the Bible to bear on life and demonstrates how it can speak to the needs of the members. Case studies help the teacher demonstrate that the Bible is timeless and that it can speak a word of instruction to people today.

A case study (the way I am using it here) is a story that has enough information for people to help solve the problem, or at least to suggest possible solutions to the problem. Sometimes these can be found in newspapers or books; other times teachers can construct their own.

A lesson that deals with ministering during the time of death needs something to get members involved rather than letting them talk about it from a distance as a philosophical concept. To introduce such a lesson read the following illustration: "Jerry and Dianne West had been married for eight years. They had two children, Boyd, age six, and Somerlie, age four. One evening on the way home from work, Dianne was killed by a drunken driver. Beverly Sharpe, Dianne's Sunday School teacher, went immediately to the home when she learned of the accident. When she arrived, the pastor was there talking to Jerry. Beverly looked around for the children. She found them upstairs in one of the bedrooms all by themselves. They were frightened and crying. Beverly put her arms around them, and they began to sob even harder. For a few minutes they all cried together.

"When they had quieted down some, she asked them what was wrong. Somerlie replied, 'Daddy said Mommie was dead. He said she had gone on a long trip to see Jesus and was never coming back. I don't want her to go see Jesus. I want her here. I don't like Jesus. I want my Mommie.'

" 'Yes,' replied Beverly. 'Your mother has died. A man who shouldn't have been driving ran into your mother's car. I'm very sad that she has died. I know it makes you sad too. Jesus is also sad that your mother has died.'

" 'She wouldn't have been killed if I had emptied the trash like she asked me to do,' sobbed Boyd. 'I really meant to do it.'

" 'Boyd,' Beverly said, 'your mother was killed because a man was driving who was not fit to drive. It had nothing to do with you. Even if you had emptied the trash, it would not have kept the man from running into your mother.'

"Beverly continued to sit with the children. Occasionally, one of them would ask some question about death or about who was going to take care of them now that their mother was dead. Beverly answered the questions as best she could, assuring the children that their father loved them and that many other people did too.

" 'When I think of your mother,' Beverly said, 'I think of how pretty she looked last Sunday morning when she sang in church. Somerlie, what is your favorite memory of your mother?' The children began the process of remembering the good things about their mother. Soon the children's grandmother arrived, and Beverly turned the children over to her."[1]

In using case studies like this, it would help if each member had a copy. After reading it aloud, ask the members to answer such questions as the following: (1) What were some illogical conclusions about death that the children had? (2) What did Beverly do right in ministering to the children? (3) What more could she have done? (4) Did she do anything that kept the children from working through their grief?

Out of a discussion of this case study, members can learn how to minister in time of death. The same principles can be given in a lecture, but in this case the members have discovered them for themselves. They will remember them far longer than if they had just been told.

Life Situations

Life situations make people think. They translate biblical teachings into modern dress. Yet, behind each of these situations lies biblical evidence and foundation.

Life situations are open-ended case studies. They can be tied closely or loosely to specific Scriptures. Their real value is in expressing the meaning of the Scripture in terms of today.

If you write your own, consider the following suggestions.

- Select a specific Scripture that you wish to use. Study the Scripture until you begin to see a particular modern situation beginning to emerge.
- Biblical stories, parables, or experiences work best in this type of activity. Passages containing narration, psalms, and historical statements would be presented best by using another method.
- You may need to modify the story slightly to keep it from being too easily recognized as a retelling of the Scripture. However, try not to introduce too many new ideas that would change the basic thrust of the biblical passage.

Use these life situations as discussion starters for a Bible study you are leading that deals with that topic or Scripture. There are no right or wrong answers to these situations.

Helping

Scripture Reference: Luke 10:25-37

Bob was out visiting for his church on Thursday evening. He had an appointment at 7:30 with a prospective family who had just moved to town. They had attended First Church for the last three Sundays, and Bob was certain they would join in spite of the fact that they had to pass First Suburban Church on the way. He glanced at his watch. He was running late. If he went around by the regular route, he would be late. He could cut through the old part of town and make it. As he drove through the dark streets, he unconsciously locked the doors of the car.

As he rounded a curve, his headlights picked up two men bending over a third man who was lying on the sidewalk. When they saw his lights, the two men broke and ran, leaving the third man on the sidewalk. Bob hesitated for a moment, trying to decide what he should do, then he. . . .

Ethical Choices

Scripture Reference: 1 Thessalonians 5:22

Bill had been a deacon in old First Church for years. He had watched the church gradually decline. He had worked with the youth for years, and they desperately needed a Christian Life Center to reach the youth of the community and to get them off the streets. One day a fellow real estate agent called him and invited him to lunch to discuss a proposal. The other agent knew Bill's involvement in the church. He suggested that he had an answer to how First Church could build the Christian Life Center. There was some property next door to the church that the agent wanted the church to buy, using its influence and its tax-exempt status and then sell it back to him. He would then make a contribution to the church so the church could build the center. No one would be hurt, it was all legal, and the kids would benefit. Bill said. . . .

Integrity, Sexual Purity

Scripture Reference: Genesis 39:1-23

Joe had met Pam when he first started working at her father's store. They had talked some at the store, when Pam called Joe and invited him to a party at her house. When he knocked, Pam met him at the door and ushered him into the den. She looked beautiful. It took Joe a minute to realize that no one else was around. He was rather confused, but he enjoyed being alone with her. After talking for a while, Pam came over and sat down in his lap. "My parents are gone for the weekend," she said. "We have the whole house to ourselves. Come on upstairs to the bedroom."

Joe was shaken. He tried to explain to Pam that he liked her a lot, but he could not have sex with her. When he continued to refuse, Pam said, "If you don't, I'll tell the police that you tried to rape me."

Joe said. . . .

Forgiveness

Scripture Reference: Genesis 37 to 45

Joe's father had divorced and remarried. From his first marriage there were several children. Joe and a younger brother had been born from the second marriage. Joe's mother had died when his younger brother was born, and his father had always favored him and his younger brother over his older stepbrothers. Needless to say, this angered the stepbrothers. Through their scheming, they were able to successfully squeeze Joe out of the family business entirely, as well as out of considerable real estate holdings.

However, Joe was a creative genius. He was successful in making some computer software that made him a considerable fortune. His brothers were not as skilled in business. One day they came to Joe and asked him for a loan. Joe said. . . .

Faithfulness, Commitment to Christ

Scripture Reference: Acts 4:1-22

Susan moved into a community that was dominated by a particular religion. She opened a store and all of the local townspeople started trading with her. They all ran up large charge accounts. One day some representatives of the religion came to talk to her. They asked her to join their church. When Susan explained that she was already an active member in her church and did not want to change, she was told that she had two choices: either convert to their religion or face bankruptcy because they would instruct their members who owed her money not to pay their bills.

Susan said. . . .

Honesty

Scripture Reference: Acts 5:1-11

Stewart and Ann had been members of First Church for several years. In an attempt to finance a massive renovation and new building, the church asked its members to make some sacrificial gifts. Several of the members had already done so. One member had sold a piece of property and had given all of the proceeds to the church. Others had given wedding rings, cars, and antiques. Stewart and Ann decided that they would sell some rental property they had in another city and tell the church they were giving all of the proceeds to the fund. However, you have a friend who is a real estate broker in that city, and you are aware of the sale price. When Stewart and Ann presented their gift to the church and said they were giving the full purchase price to the church, you said. . . .

Courage, Convictions

Scripture Reference: Esther 3:1 to 7:10
Judy had just been hired as a vice-president in charge of marketing for a large textile firm. She had not been on the job long when one of her employees came to her with a problem. According to the employee, some of the other employees had a scheme going. They would take the expensive fabric that was being shipped to makers of designer dresses and substitute inferior material that was made in the same design. They then sold the more expensive material and pocketed the profit. The former vice-president had learned of the scheme and threatened to expose it. The guilty employees had threatened him and his family with bodily harm. Rather than face the issue, the man had asked for a transfer. When Judy learned of this situation, she said. . . .

Twenty Questions

Playing twenty questions is just another way to study the Scripture by making it a little more enjoyable. It is nothing more than twenty questions that have been made up to cover the facts in a certain passage of Scripture. You can ask group members to read the passage, then have them close their Bibles and see if they can answer the questions. You can use the questions at the beginning as a pretest; you can use them at the end as a posttest; or you can use them in both places to see how much the group learned in the Bible session.

You can make questions easy or difficult. You can ask just for facts or for meanings of Scriptures and interpretations. Fit your degree of difficulty to your audience and what you want to accomplish.

Jesus Heals a Blind Man

Scripture References: Luke 18:35-43 (Matt. 20:29-34; Mark 10:46-52)
  1. Where was Jesus when this encounter occurred? (Jericho)
  2. What was the man's name that he met? (Bartimaeus)

3. What was wrong with him? (He was blind.)
4. What did he do to earn a living? (begged)
5. Where did the encounter take place? (roadside)
6. How did Bartimaeus know Jesus was coming? (heard the crowd)
7. What title did Bartimaeus use to refer to Jesus? (Son of David)
8. What implications did using that title have? (messianic)
9. What was the crowd's reaction to Bartimaeus? (tried to silence him)
10. How did Bartimaeus respond to the crowd's silencing? (called louder)
11. How did Bartimaeus appeal to Jesus? (asked for mercy)
12. What was Jesus' reaction to Bartimaeus's call? (ordered him to be brought to Him)
13. What did Jesus ask Bartimaeus? (What do you want me to do for you?)
14. Why do you think Jesus asked this question? (their answers)
15. What did Bartimaeus want? (to see)
16. What did Jesus do for him? (healed him)
17. What did Jesus say made Bartimaeus well? (his own faith)
18. What was Bartimaeus' immediate reaction? (praised God)
19. How did Bartimaeus respond later? (followed Jesus)
20. What was the crowd's reaction? (praised God)

Puzzles and Games

Learning can be fun. Biblical puzzles and games can help people learn even while they are having fun. This section of learning activities is a little different than the others in this book. However, it can be as useful in planning exciting learning activities as the others. You will just use these in a little different way.

Puzzles can be used in several different ways. They are great to begin a learning activity, such as a Bible study group or a Sunday School class. Prepare one of the puzzles and place on all the chairs before the group arrives. As they enter, ask them to begin working the puzzle immediately. This way those who arrive early are rewarded for their promptness. This can also encourage the perennial latecomers to be on time. (I said *encourage;* that's all you can do. Some people will never be on time. But whatever you do, don't wait to begin until they arrive and don't take the group's time to fill them in on what you have done when they do come in late. Don't penalize those who arrive on time.)

For these early activities, any of the puzzles work well. A crossword puzzle or a word search puzzle drawn directly from the passage of Scripture you are studying can familiarize group members with the passage you are going to study.

Don't hesitate to use games when you have the opportunity. People can learn and not even be aware of it.

Consider these suggestions if you write your own:

- Keep the complexity of the puzzle in line with the amount of time you have available for its use. A full-sized crossword puzzle cannot be worked in five minutes as a beginning activity. However, a crossword puzzle that requires only five or six answers or a word search puzzle would work well in this situation.

- Be sure your puzzles are correct. Nothing is more frustrating for those working it, and embarrassing for the one who has prepared it, than to find that there is an error in it. Proofread carefully.

- Unless your group is quite experienced in working crossword puzzles, keep them simple. Remember your purpose is to have them learn facts out of the Bible, not see if you can stump their crossword puzzle working ability.

People and Places in Jeremiah[2]

Scripture Reference: Jeremiah 40:1 to 45:5

```
J  O  H  A  N  A  N  D
Z  E  G  Y  P  T  J  A
B  A  R  U  C  H  I  W
G  I  B  E  O  N  M  N
X  I  S  H  M  A  E  L
G  E  D  A  L  I  A  H
M  I  C  J  U  D  A  H
B  F  M  I  Z  P  A  H
```

Johanan, Egypt, Jeremiah, Gibeon, Ishmael, Gedaliah, Judah, Mizpah.

Scripture Word Search Puzzle[3]

Scripture Reference: 2 Peter 1:19-20

Fill in the blanks in the following verses and then find the words in the puzzle.

"We have also a more _____ _____ of _____; whereunto ye do well that ye take _____, as unto a _____ that _____ in a _____ place, until the _____ _____ and the day _____ arise in your _____: Knowing this _____ that no prophecy of the _____ is of any _____ _____."

```
I  A  T  S  E  P  E  H
N  W  A  D  S  R  I  F
T  H  G  I  L  I  U  U
E  E  I  N  D  V  T  S
R  E  S  T  R  A  E  H
P  H  E  A  D  T  R  W
R  R  W  C  A  E  U  K
E  H  O  Y  R  A  T  S
T  T  R  P  O  P  P  E
A  E  D  Y  H  R  I  S
T  N  V  C  E  E  R  D
I  I  I  I  E  O  C  A
O  H  R  F  D  W  S  Y
N  S  P  T  S  R  I  F
```

Topical Word Search Puzzle[4]

Scripture Reference: 1 Peter 4:3

```
D  I  S  I  D  R  U  K  N  S  N
Y  J  E  T  S  S  I  G  R  O  Y
R  T  K  S  E  R  D  K  I  N  T
T  Y  I  I  N  D  O  T  N  U  O
A  S  G  L  S  S  A  N  S  S  S
L  R  U  T  A  P  L  U  S  U  U
O  N  R  O  I  U  T  R  S  S  L
D  S  D  S  L  K  S  D  I  I  L
I  I  S  T  I  D  O  N  D  D  O
S  I  U  I  T  Y  L  U  E  S  D
D  R  U  N  K  E  N  N  E  S  S
```

In the above puzzle are hidden six sins that characterized the believer before he was saved. Read 1 Peter 4:3 and then see if you can find the following words: *sensuality, lust, drunkenness, orgies, dissipation, idolatry.*

Study Guide

Scripture Reference: Esther 3:2,5-6; 4:13-16; 7:3-6a
(Designed to be used with the biblical simulation, "Esther Saves Her People.")

Group 1.—Please read Esther 3:2,5-6 and answer the following questions.

1. To what position did King Xerxes appoint Haman and what did he order the people to do? _____

2. Why did Mordecai not bow down to Haman?_____

3. What was Haman's reaction to Mordecai's refusal to bow down?

Group 2.—Please Read Esther 4:13-16 and answer the following questions.

1. What argument did Mordecai use to urge Esther to speak out? ___

2. Would God have been able to save the Jews without Esther's help?

3. Why did Mordecai feel that Esther had been made queen? _____

4. What did Esther ask Mordecai and the Jews to do? _____

Group 3.—Please read Esther 7:3-6*a* and answer the following questions.
1. By referring to the background passage, what did Esther do to speak to the king? _____

2. What did Esther ask the king? _____

3. What happened to Haman? _____

Notes

1. James E. Taulman, *Encouragers: The Sunday School Worker's Counseling Ministry* (Nashville: Broadman Press, 1986), pp. 53-54. Used by permission.

2. *Bible Book Study for Adult Teachers: Resource Kit,* Kit Item 14 (Nashville: The Sunday School Board of the Southern Baptist Convention), July-September, 1985. Used by permission.

3. *Bible Book Study Guide* (Nashville: The Sunday School Board of the Southern Baptist Convention), July-September, 1984, p. 37. Used by permission.

4. Ibid., p. 20. Used by permission.

Topical Index

Scripture Index

127